OUT OF THE ASHES: A REDEFINED ME

WRITTEN BY

LaKecia Lanier

And

DEDICATED TO

TO MY GRANDMOTHERS
GENNELL MCKINSEY AND IRENE JACKSON

Table of Contents

FORWARD   3

ACKNOWLEDGEMENTS   4

PREFACE   6

WHO ARE YOU?   9

DEAD ENDS   25

BONDAGE   49

CONSUMING FIRE   64

OUT OF THE ASHES   81

LaKecia G. Lanier, my eldest child is a gift from God. I have watched her grow from a little girl into a God Fearing Women. As a young girl, she was raised in the church and she had a love for ministry.

The Holy Spirit has totally transformed her life! Her ministry and transparency, has blessed so many women of all ethnicities. This book **"Out of The Ashes: A Redefined Me"** will tremendously bless you.

Allow the Holy Spirit to minister to you, heal you and restore you into the child of God he has destined you to be.

As God has done it for LaKecia, He will do the same thing for you!

Restoration today is your Portion!

Apostle Gloria J. Scutchins

As you read this book **Out of The Ashes** you will find a powerful testimony of Deliverance, Perseverance, Healing and Triumph. Lakecia speaks to many facts of life that many share but have not ascertained how to make their exit from one stage of life to the next. As you read you will find the path to your personal triumph and will establish the New & **Redefined You!!**

James E. Scutchins, Sr.

ACKNOWLEDGEMENTS

To my husband Corrie.. I adore you! Words cannot express my love for you. My love for you flows from such a deep place. You are what God embodied just for me. Thank you for your support, your faithfulness and for loving ALL of me.

To my momma Gloria… You have prayed and pushed me to grow and go forward. Thank you for believing in me. Thank you for grooming me. If I have never said how much I appreciate you, I say it now! I honor you.

To my three sons, (Arkeen, Michael, and Ethan)…Mommy loves you all so much. I am grateful for you three. You three make my world complete. Everything that I have done to better myself, I did it because I wanted to be better for you!

To my daddy Charles.. I am FOREVER daddy's baby girl.

To my pa-pa,-James Scutchins Sr., My siblings Ken (Berg-O), Imani (Cleo), and James Jr (JayR)... I love you and constantly pray for you!

To the *Firm (Latrisha, Qiana, Kewanda, Seanelle, and Lisa)…* You ladies held me down when I needed you all the most. I will never forget it. I am forever grateful for your love, your truth and friendship…

To Johnny… Thank You for your support and your never-ending loyalty.

To my Shekinah Doxa Family.. I love you all. Thank you for standing with me and encouraging me. Thank you for praying for me. You are the best church on this side of heaven.

[4]

Special Thanks to Tia and Neki- I love you both so much. You both mean so much to me. Thank you for your support. There have been so many other people who have supported my work and contributed to making this book happen. Thank you so very much! Everything that you have done for me is appreciated.

"I will Praise thee for I am FEARFULLY and WONDERFULLY made; marvelous are thy works; and that my soul knoweth right well" (Psalms 139:14 KJV)

You ARE fearfully and wonderfully made! You have been shaped *first* inside and then out; you were formed in your mother's womb. You are BREATHTAKING—body and soul!! God knows exactly WHO YOU ARE! He knows every hair on your head. He knows what you are thinking before you think it. He knows the choices you make before you make them. (Yes, even the ones that He would frown upon.)And YET He still blesses you… Yet He still calls you HIS. Yet, He still calls you beautiful... He STILL pursues you….

This book is geared toward women from all walks of life. However, I am aware that some may not be able to identify with my story, and that is okay. There are women who have suffered as I have and gone through various situations in their lives that have left them feeling desperate and depleted. These situations have left them feeling hopeless. These are women who have looked for something that seemed to be so far out of their reach… that one thing that seems unobtainable.

I want to encourage those women who are in that situation RIGHT now. I want you to know that our Father God is willing to fill that void. He is willing to do what is necessary to DELIVER you from those things that oppress you as well as DELIVER you from yourself!!
"For I know the thoughts that I think towards you, saith the Lord, thoughts of Peace, and not of evil, to give you an EXPECTED end.

I would often wonder about this statement. We hear it so many times and it begins to sound redundant and more like a cliché often times than not. When we come into the knowledge of who GOD really is we understand that ALL he does, he does for HIS glory. The expected end is our victory but it is for his Glory!! LaKecia hasn't done anything spectacular, but I thank God for his mercy and his Grace. Without them both, I don't know where I would be.

I'm BETTER because of my PROCESS!! I am better because I went through the fire and my ashes speak for me. My ashes are a product of my testimony. In my resilience to life's situations, I've learned how to weather the storms. To bend but not to break...

What does it mean to be REDIFINED? Redefine simply means to give something a new meaning or to change something. In 2008, my life was forever changed and altered by the power of the Holy Spirit. I want to share the journey with you. This book is not a tell all neither is it a book that would place blame on anyone else. Instead, it is about ME, MY LIFE, and MY PERCEPTONS. I alone take full responsibility for my actions and decisions that I have made in my life. I AM NOT A VICTIM but I AM A SURVIVOR!!

It is an honor to write this book. I couldn't wait another year to compete it. I was filled with anxiety and trepidation prior to finishing it because I was so concerned about what others would say when they read it. I was worried about what others would think about my experiences. I was worried about what my children would think of their mother.

However, I was led by the Holy Spirit in everything that I disclosed, so I know that the book is ready!! I am READY!! The Lord impressed upon me an urgency to complete the work that HE has already started. This book comes from my heart and my soul; to give you a realistic view of how God can save and deliver. If he did it for me he will do the same thing for you…

"But you are a chosen generation, a royal priesthood, a holy nation, a peculiar people; that ye should shew forth the praises of him who hath called you out of the darkness into the marvelous light" (1 Peter 2:9)"

Who are you? Many women can't answer this question. Sometimes we lose ourselves in relationships, in the daily cycle of our lives, and in the perception of others. Until you know who you are, you will remain in the place that you are in; whether or not it's a loveless relationship or a mundane life. You cannot discover who you are without reflecting on the things that make you, YOU. If you don't know who you are how can you love who you are?

And if you can't love who you are then how can you love someone else? I can recall watching a movie called the *"Runaway Bride"* with Julia Roberts. Every time she got with a new man she would change her preference of how she ate her eggs. It wasn't until one day after a relationship was over that she sat down and discovered the type of eggs she liked! It can be as simple as that. What is it that you like to do? What types of food do you like? What's your favorite color? *"We are so accustomed to disguising ourselves to others that in the end we become disguised to ourselves."*(Francois De La Rochefoucauld)

Many women jump from one man to another without allowing themselves to heal. With the death of anything should be a mourning period. Give yourself time to mourn the death of the relationship. It is necessary. Some people think that to get OVER the situation you must get INTO another. That's so untrue. When you do that, you are starting the relationship with baggage (which includes soul ties) and with a shaky foundation. This relationship ends up being a rebound and therefore has problems from the start.

Trust me, I know. I have done this exact thing so many times. I have seen myself in this very situation so many times.

When you allow yourself time to be by yourself, you can discover who you really are. Some women don't like to be by their selves because they don't like the person that they have become! You don't like the stillness or the quietness that make you take a look at yourself. You don't want to see that perhaps you are the cause of so many failed relationships. You don't want to examine why you are so mean and nasty.

Why are you so domineering and aggressive? *"I'm an independent woman and I don't need A man"* Right!! Perhaps this is the reason why you don't have one! If you have said that, chances are you don't know your place. What man wants an aggressive woman? Why are you so needy? Every relationship you have, you cling to for dear life, afraid of rejection and unsure about yourself.

Our baggage has shaped our attitudes and eventually our lives. The way we treat our children and our significant others can be derived from the baggage of failed relationships. "You look just like your father!" how many of us have said that with distaste in our mouths? How sad is that?! Examine YOURSELF and ask God to help you change. This book is going to cause you to reflect on you.

I have discovered that when I didn't like something about myself I would harp on it until it became bigger than what it really was. For example, when I was a child I hated that I had dark skin. My mother and my brother are both of a lighter complexion. Dark Skinned girls were NOT happening back in the 80s. I was very aware of my skin color. It was brought up by friends whenever I wanted to wear certain colors *"that won't look good on you because your skin is so dark."*

I felt so inferior to other people. I felt that no one really looked at me past my dark skin.

As a young girl and feeling like I was not considered pretty like my light-skinned friends or family members, this was a horrible thing to live through. I was discriminated against in my very own culture and race. I was made to feel like my dark skin was not beautiful. I felt like I didn't fit in at school, home or anywhere else where lighter people were considered fairer people.

I thought that I was unattractive and that no one would really want me or want to get to know me because my skin was so dark, it didn't help that I was a late developer, so I was straight as a board. I had no curves whatsoever. I also had thick lips and very small eyes. As a matter of fact, one of my eyes had a very lazy eye lid and would droop. I didn't like to look at myself much and hoped others wouldn't look at me either. I tried to blend in with my surroundings and not be noticed by others. I would sit in the back of the room or in corners of the room where no one would really look to see me. With this growing complex of my skin and my features, came many other issues. But it stemmed from the way I looked and what society deemed was beautiful.

Because of this issue I had with my physical attributes, my self-esteem was not up to par. I suffered badly because of poor decisions I made. I became sexual at an early age. I had my first boyfriend at the age of 16 years old. He was older than me and I believe now really didn't care too much about me. But of course, you couldn't tell me he didn't love me. When people would tell me the truth about him and what they knew he was doing, I would adamantly deny any wrong doing on his behalf. Isn't that like some of us, ladies?

People try to tell us when we are headed for disaster but we don't want to believe it. We see the signs of an abuser, or a cheater, or poor provider but we stay anyways, hoping that we can change him? I'm sorry, but no woman (I don't care how good her sex, cooking, or She is) can change a man! A person changes when they want to!! No one has the capability to change another human being.

I am convinced that when all women realize who we are, we will change society. Our standards would be higher because we recognize that we are Queens and should be treated as such. When we come to recognize who we are, we will DEMAND a certain level of respect. For example, sleeping around with a man that is not your husband. How do you expect him to respect you when your foundation is based on a lie? How could you ever trust that individual when you know how you started?

Yes we have heard of people marrying those they cheated on their spouses with, but if those same people would tell the truth, I believe they would tell you that trust is a major issue in their relationship! Raise your standards and watch how men change for the better.

I was in this relationship at 16 years old, with this older more experienced young man. He was very popular at school and all the girls loved him. I was amazed that he would even consider me. We also went to the same local church. I was able to see him more than the girls at school.

You can imagine my surprise when we began to get closer and began dating. I was surprised that he even looked at me with my thick unibrow and thin shape. Many other people were surprised as well. I recall my friends at the time questioning his choice in me. Soon after we started to date we began having sex.

My mother found out and banned him from seeing me. That didn't matter. When she went to work I would sneak him in the house and we would be together there. I began to skip school on the regular just so I could be with him. He was a senior so he had more of a flexible schedule that I did. A few months into the relationship, I found out that he was cheating on me with a girl that was much prettier than me and more popular. AND she was light-skinned. What a blow to my psyche!

I was devastated. But by this time I was pregnant. I couldn't even bring myself to tell him. I thought he would think I was trying to trap him or pull him away from the girl that he eventually chose to be with. So one day, I again skipped school and after having stolen my medical insurance card from my mother, I prepared to have an abortion. I walked through the throng of protestors with their horrible signs of butchered fetuses and walked into the office. I was so ashamed.

Every time that my name was called, I looked across the room to see if anyone was looking at me. I was looking to see if I saw anyone who may know my mother or me. There was a dark wood door that females of all ages would walk through and not come back. I knew that when you got called to go behind that door, you would not be leaving this building the same way that you came in.

I was so ashamed that I had gotten myself into this situation and I was alone to deal with it. When the nurse called my name for the final time to go behind the dark wood door, my knees were shaking. I was trembling under my winter coat.

She brought me into a cozy room with a rocking chair in it. It had pretty colors and was very warm but I was still shaking. As the nurse told me to change into the gown that was left on the very thin bed, tears were streaming down my face. I will never forget how the nurse grabbed me by the hand, and told me that there have been thousands of girls before me who have had this same procedure done.

I think she wanted me to feel better, but it made me feel worse. It made me feel worse that young women had felt this same exact way that I was feeling at this moment. As I stripped from the waist down and put the gown on I was really looking for another way out. I was analyzing the situation I was in. I was trying to think of other options. But in my young mind, there were none! They wheeled me into another room that was cold and sterile. I could not see the doctor's faces because they had on surgical masks over their mouths. I thought that I was in a nightmare.

I had seen scenes like this on the television. I can remember tears running down my face as the anesthesiologist told me to count to ten. When I woke up my baby was gone.
I felt so bereft. I was so empty. What did I do? Why did I just kill my baby? How did this baby that I didn't even acknowledge begin to mean so much to me? I knew I had done something terrible.

My mind was reeling from what I just did to my body. Somewhere on a deeper level, I knew I had crossed some spiritual boundaries. I knew that I had done wrong on so many deeper levels. I had no one to tell; No one that I trusted enough to share this with.

I was grieving badly and I was hurt. I was hurt by the decision I had to make and the fact that I was indeed all alone. As I rode the city bus home alone, I cried so much the other passengers were staring.

I did not know then that teen abortion is linked to physical and psychological problems including drug and alcohol abuse, suicide attempts and ideation, and other self-destructive behaviors. 20% of abortions in the U.S are performed on teens. Currently 24 out of every 1,000 teen have an abortion.

This means that every year 200,000 teens have abortions. Compared to older women, teens are significantly more likely to report severe emotional injuries related to their abortion. Teens who have had abortions are more likely to get pregnant again in an effort to replace the baby they aborted. So if the young woman does not get help, the cycle may continue. (www.teenpregnancystatistics.org)

This was not the end of the relationship between the young man and me. I continued to be foolish and stood by as he slept with those I called friends. This relationship was the second relationship that changed the way I viewed men, relationships and people in general.

I never talked about the experience of the abortion until I was asked to speak as an inspirational speaker at a Women's conference. It wasn't planned neither was it in my notes. However, I was obedient to the Holy Spirit and many women were set free. Several of them came to me after the service, thanking me for sharing and acknowledging similar experiences. There are so many women who have experienced abortions and have not told anyone. They are holding on to the shame and the feelings of guilt that accompany those memories. If that is you reading this passage, I beseech you to ask for forgiveness from our heavenly Father.

Express your repentance and allow the Holy Spirit to cleanse your mind and your heart from those feelings of turmoil and guilt. I want you to be healed. To have kept that secret so long and then finally to have released it, felt so good to me. Find someone that you can trust. Go to your pastor or a leader of your church that you trust and release it to them.

If you are not a part of a church, then find a good friend that won't judge you. Someone that understands the importance of you releasing these weights from your mind and heart. God is just waiting for you to release it. He has already forgiven you and He loves you in spite of. It's time to be FREE!! In Jesus' name!

The first relationship that every young girl has is with her father-the one who helped with her conception. The father-daughter relationship is very important in the development of the daughter. This is her first male-female relationship and will influence her behavior with her husband later in life. It will influence all her other relationships as well. The earliest reflection (insight) of herself will come from her dad. How does Daddy view me? Does he accept me without reservations? Does Daddy love me even though my skin is dark?

When a father shows his daughter respect she feels worthwhile and like a princess but when he ignores her or doesn't spend enough time with her or is too critical of her, she feels worthless. She feels rejected and hence starts the cycle of insecurities. A father is supposed to be there to show love to his daughter.

The love she receives from her father would help her in the years to come. She won't settle for anything less than the kind nurturing love she has already received. A father should be around to take his daughter out, and to assist in teaching her the ways of the world. It is his job to make sure she is secure in herself.

When a female is secure within herself, there are certain things she will just not do. She won't allow a man to cheat on her and take him back. She won't allow him to beat her and take him back. She will value herself and wait until God PRESENTS her to her Adam.   When a female has a father in her life, she is less prone to seek male attention.

What is worse than a busy woman who craves attention? There are so many issues with that. The woman who craves attention won't stop at anything until she gets it. That makes her manipulative, selfish and even competitive and jealous.

A young woman is less likely to be sexually active at an early age because she has the love of her father to fill the void that his absence would make. Young girls measure every other male in her life to her father. Because so many of our families in the African American community are broken, many young girls are being raised by their mothers. I fell into this category. My mother and my father were young when they conceived me. My mother was 18 years old when she gave birth to me. While living in upstate New York my dad helped her raise me but when we moved to Hartford, Connecticut I lost my daddy.

He didn't move with us (for reasons I am unsure about) and momma had to raise me on her own. He would eventually tell me that he did come to Connecticut ready to be with my mother and to help raise me but she sent him away because she had started a new life.

We have kept in contact with each other throughout the years but the relationship is not where I would have wanted it to be. I regret that. However, I felt that it was too late to capture what was lost so many years ago. I do not hate my daddy. Just the opposite. I love him so much. I wish things had been different between us back then. There had been times when I was at my worse and I wished I'd had my daddy.

There were times when I would cry myself to sleep because I wished I'd had my daddy. Not really knowing him but knowing enough to want to be near him was my issue. When I would see him in the summers or whenever I could, I would stay very close to him. People would see him and they would see me right there. I was Daddy's baby girl. He still calls me that. Whenever I call him, he is there. If I need anything he will give it if he can. I just wished that I've had access to him all my life. When I needed him the most, I wish he had just been there.

I needed him throughout my adolescent years. I needed him to love on me and show me how special I was. But I understand now, that life happens. As adults, we make decisions that affect the children we have. I remember going to New York for the summer. My daddy bought me a brand new bike. Well, I didn't know how to ride a bike without training wheels. My dad was washing his truck on the grass and playing his music one summer evening. I recall wanting to ride that bike more than anything.

My step-sisters were riding theirs and I wanted to be able to ride just as well. I recall my daddy noticing me struggling to get on and ride. He stopped washing his truck and came to help me on my bike. He held onto the back of the bike as I began to peddle. My heart swelled in my chest as I began to balance on my own.

He held on for a little while longer, running behind me. Then he let go!! I was riding my bike on my own. I was cruising and it felt so good. That was all I needed-the help from my daddy. I turned my bike around to come back down the sidewalk. As I got closer to his truck, I began to wobble a bit.

Before I knew it, I had crashed into his truck and scratched his paint with my handlebar. I was very upset and afraid of the consequence from that. I just knew I was going to get in trouble. But no-My daddy told me it was okay. As he held me close, he told me that as long as I was alright he was alright.

That's when I knew as a little girl that I was missing something on a much higher level. I knew that when I went back to Connecticut, I would be leaving this man. I would be leaving his love, his acceptance, and his ability to make me feel special. Even though I was one of a few children in the house, my daddy also gave me individualized attention.

Those feelings that I had shared with my dad, would be the same ones I would continue to search for as an adult. I was hurt and jealous that others had my father and I only got to see him certain times of the year. I carried that hurt and jealousy for many years and I allowed it to drive a wedge between my father and me. I allowed it to drive a wedge between me and my paternal side of the family. With the issues that I had with these two prominent relationships in my early years I was left feeling unfulfilled and searching for my identity. I was lost. There were walls that I built to protect myself from ever getting hurt again; Walls that my husband and I are still tearing down.

During this period, I was often alone. I wanted relationships but was too afraid to start them. I began to just "live in my head." I loved to read books and would often fantasize of another life for myself. Depression was my friend. Depression and suicidal thoughts accompanied me on a daily basis. I recall thinking that if I would just kill myself, things would be better for everyone else around me. If I would just do it then I could put myself out of my misery. I wouldn't have to feel so alone anymore. I wouldn't have to feel so isolated and so desperate to be loved. I wouldn't have to feel anything anymore, because I would be dead. I would battle with this spirit for many years afterwards.

Depression is a spirit that chases me. It desires for me to give up and kill myself. When I was a teenager, I remember thinking that I was going to either kill myself or be committed to a mental asylum. I'm grateful to God that I am still in my

[19]

right mind and depression and suicidal thoughts are behind me.

If you are struggling with depression and suicidal thoughts, I want you to know that God loves you and you are not alone. God wants to heal your mind and restore you. He cares for you! He is concerned about his children.

Talk to someone about your issues. Seek help! There is nothing wrong with psychiatric help! I am a firm believer in the fact that doctors were put on this earth with specific abilities to assist God's people with obtaining healing. But it's according to your faith! Do you want to be healed and restored?

Due to feeling like I was unfulfilled I was promiscuous. Regardless of who I was with, I was still searching. I was still battling with the inner me, battling with my identity, searching for fulfillment with men. I never felt complete. I never really felt accepted or loved.

As I grew older my thoughts were to use men just like they used me. I thought that if I kept someone in my life, I wouldn't have to deal with me. People tend to focus on other's issues so that they don't have to deal with their own. I was hurting and I had no one around me that could reach me. There were so many events that led to this behavior. Like being sexually abused while on summer vacation in my early teens and constantly being depressed.

I hurt because I didn't let anyone in. I was hurting because I was tired of getting hurt by the people who I thought would never hurt me. I was hurting because I seemed so invisible! I wanted to be seen. I wanted people to like me. I was searching for acceptance by the people I went to church with, my family, associates and my parents- especially my mother.

As much as I ADORE my mother now, the relationship between my mother and me (as a teenager and young adult) was very strained. She would say that when I got into junior high that I took a turn for the worse. However, our strenuous relationship started when my brother was born. My brother and I are seven years apart. His father and his family were very active in his life. I can remember how on the holidays he would come home with garbage bags full of toys and clothes. I was very jealous of my brother. He had a family that loved him very much while I had only my mother most of the time.

He had a family that would call and check on him. They would call to speak with him. But I didn't have my daddy calling and asking for me. Neither did I have any of his family calling for me. He also had light skin like my mother and his father. In my mind, he was her favorite. She coddled him and soon I felt rejected by my mom. Of course in retrospect, I know my mother wasn't showing favoritism. He was and is the baby. But still, as a youth this bothered me on so many different levels.

Every time I was being disciplined I would hear her say "I wish you could be more like your brother... your brother doesn't give me such a hard time like you do. He doesn't talk back...etc." The comparison of the two of us only pushed me further away. {*These feelings towards my brother eventually went away as I matured. For a while it was my brother, my mother and I until she married. It was us against the world. Needless to say, my brother is a sparkle in my eye and I am proud of the man he has grown to be.*} The jealousy and the hatred of my younger brother grew until I remember wanting to hurt him.

I recall watching him in church choking on a peppermint ball. I just sat there and watched him. He had his hands around his throat and his eyes were huge as he tried to get Momma's attention. Eventually, she noticed him and some way or another the peppermint ball was extracted from his throat.

As previously mentioned, my mother was a faithful member of one of the local churches. At one time she was Youth President and all the young people loved her. I couldn't stand her. I felt that she gave all her time to church and my brother. I felt that she never tried to understand me.

We could never have a conversation and have it end peacefully with either agreement or agreeing to disagree. She was always in her bible or praying. If she wasn't doing that, then she was dragging us to church-literally. I did not want to go. However, every time that church opened we were there and usually some of the first ones.

Because of how I felt towards her and my brother, I would often run away from home, only to come back soon after. One time she threatened to call my dad and report to him my behavior in school and at home. I really didn't care because to me, he wasn't there anyways so what he had to say did not matter. I rebelled against everything that she tried to implement. Every rule, I broke it. I was not concerned about punishments, because she never stuck to them. I made life very hard for my mother.

I began to have suicidal thoughts again. My first suicide attempt was when I swallowed pills only to wake up the next morning with no physical harm done. I thought that my family would be better off without me. I knew the hard work my mother was putting in to provide for my brother and me. She was doing her best to raise me. However, society and its norms were against her.

There is a phenomenon called the *Feminization of Poverty*. This theory basically states that women represent a disproportionate percentage of the world's poor. It reflects the consequence of lack of income as well as the deprivation of capabilities in society. So although my mother tried her best to give me the best, the odds were against her. Looking back in retrospect, I am so grateful that she raised me the way she did. ***Train up a child in the way he should go: and when he is old, he will not depart from it (proverbs 22:6).***

My mother instilled in me the basics of my Christian foundation; the fundamentals. She taught me how to pray. When I found myself in situations later explained in this book, it was the teachings she provided as well as her Godly example that provided a way out.

For the reasons of rejection, low self-esteem, depression, and many other issues, suicide was a constant thought. Depression was a constant battle. I began to believe the thoughts that said I would die in a mental institution. I thought that I should kill myself and save my family the embarrassment of putting me in an institution. But I knew that wasn't the way out. Something inside of me told me to hold on a little while longer. You ever been there? So tired of the blows of life and the constant chaos it renders? Sick and tired of being sick and tired.

Here I was a young woman and already sick of dealing with life. I'm already sick of having to save face for church and the people in my inner circle. As a young woman I learned early how to wear a mask. Life circumstances taught me how to wear a mask. I was hurting but no one knew any better. I was singing in the choir, attending Sunday school and hurting. I was singing with a girl group and was invisible. No one could see me. Everyone believed the mask that I wore.

They bought into the facade that I created. I understand now that many of these same people that I expected to recognize what I was going through were wearing masks themselves. I was tired of being something that I wasn't and I was dying slowly. But something inside of me wouldn't let me give up. I know it gets hard sometimes but we must remember *"Weeping may endure for a night but Joy comes in the morning"*. **(Psalms 30:5)**. I declare that as you are reading this book your MORNING is here!!

I declare and decree that there are no more mental chains holding you hostage in the matchless name of Jesus Christ our Lord!!! I pray that you are FREE in the name of Jesus Christ from every spirit that tortures and torments you! You know that you are MORE than a Conqueror through him that loves you.

As previously stated those two relationships with men caused serious damage to me as a young woman. The absence of my daddy and the rejection and humiliation of my first relationship devastated me and forever changed my life. They started a cycle that I was not able to break until I was in my thirties and married the love of my life. However, I still deal with remnants of the hurt and the rejection. I still have to tear down walls of isolation, mistrust and fear to start relationships,. A fear to trust people. I preferred to be alone and by myself because I knew I wouldn't hurt myself. I wouldn't betray myself. I wouldn't damage myself. But in the end, I was damaging myself by holding myself hostage from feeling loved by anyone that was around me.

I wanted the wrong type of love. I thought that the intimate version *(Eros)* love was what I needed. But no, I needed the AGAPE. The love that ABBA Father shows us on a daily basis. I didn't understand that type of love- love that covered a multiple of sins. Love that is patient, gentle and is kind. I would not experience this love until I was an adult and married my husband.

We must understand that life is only found in a relationship ordained by God. For example, relationships with your family and your parents should bring you a satisfying life. A relationship between husband and wife should be one that brings life. The Bible states that *"**the wages of sin is death**"* (Romans 6:23) any relationship that has sin in it (or developed because of sin) is prone to death. Women, this is a good example of why it is so important to wait until marriage before indulging in sex. You don't want to endanger your relationship by coercing with sin and therefore bringing death.

If you want your marriage to be one of health and life then you should refrain from all sexual activities. Refrain from everything that would displease God as you are being prepared for your predestined day. Even cohabitation (living together) before marriage, can cause a disruption in the divine order of God's plan. It is not his plan that men and women divorce; especially Christians.

Did you know that couples who lived together before marriage, tend to divorce early in their marriage? Did you know that only 50% of couples who were cohabitating before marriage actually got married? (Familystudies.org)Wouldn't you want to start your relationship off right and avoid a dead end?

As I went through my high school years, I was still a lost young woman that was sitting in the church pew with my own demons. By this time my mother was an Evangelist and was still very active in the church. It appeared that she was so faithful to the church but had no time for me. I can recall asking myself "how can she love this God so much that she never seen, yet her very own flesh and blood she ignores or refuses to relate too?" This caused major strain in our relationship.

I didn't talk to her about anything at all. I began to internalize and I refused to talk about anything of importance to her. As a preacher's kid I was not allowed to go to any parties. I can remember running away to go to a house party. My mother and my aunt came looking for me along with the police. I was so embarrassed.

I can remember how I was skipping school once and got arrested for trespassing on private property. My mother had to come and bail me out of jail. I continued with this behavior until she finally had enough of me and put me out. At this time, I began living with my God-father and a friend of his.

My God-father was a great man. He cared for me when it seemed as though no one else did.

He would often sit up with me and listen to me ramble into the wee hours of the night about high-school, and about life in general. He would tell me that above all he just wanted to see me by successful. He would tell me that I was so smart, I could do anything that I wanted in life. My God-father would remind me that I didn't have to settle. He was a father figure to me in many ways.

His friend was an older woman that was not originally from the area. She seemed to be the only one besides my God-father who would listen to me. I felt like I could talk to her about anything. She was very nurturing and catered to my every whim.

I found myself getting very close to her. She soon made her intentions known and for a while I refused her advances. I knew that kind of a relationship was wrong. It went against everything that I had been taught. Woman was made for man.

I had never battled with this type of thing before. I was NOT the child that can say I have always desired same sex relationships. No that was not me. That was not my issue growing up but because of my vulnerability and because of the rejection and the low self-esteem I had for myself, what was taboo became welcomed.

Eventually, the advances, her attention and her charm wore me down. She gave me the attention that I sought after. She promised to always be there for me. She took care of me. That was a void that I had. I was calling out for attention. I wanted a meaningful relationship with someone who could reciprocate the love I had for them.

[27]

I didn't realize until later in my life (when I had a one on one experience with the Holy Spirit) that the only being that can fill that void is Jesus Christ. However, I found myself in an intimate relationship with this woman. And when I did that, my life really spiraled out of control.

I separated myself from my family due to the shame. I dropped out of school because I didn't want my friends to know. I stopped going to church. I dared not step into the house of the Lord knowing that I was in a relationship with this woman. See- I was raised to believe that God was so scary I deemed him to be a boogey man.

In actuality, God is just the opposite. He is a loving, compassionate, merciful, faithful Father. I really believe that if the Body of Christ would extend the same loving-kindness that He extends to us, we could win more souls-adding to His Kingdom. This method would be more effective than preaching hate across the pulpit.

No one really explained to me that God's grace doesn't go away because of choices we make. His love for me never wavered because I was in this relationship. No he loved me in spite of. He did not love my mess-my sin. But he loved me!

The guilt that I wore was thick and tangible like a cloak. I was mad at the world because I felt stuck in this relationship. Stuck because although I didn't want to be in it, I didn't want to leave it. In my mind, she was giving me what I needed-even though I knew it was wrong.

Everything that I knew I should be doing stopped because of my lifestyle. I was extremely guilty and ashamed. There was no pleasure or gratification that came from that relationship because I had no peace. God would not allow me to have peace in something that was totally contrary to His will for me. There was a war going on for my life, for my mind and for my

[28]

spirit. This is how the enemy tricks us. We become so reliant and dependent on our desires and appetites we lose focus on what is RIGHT before God.

I felt like I was desperately losing. I know now that this was a spiritual battle for *we wrestle not against flesh and blood but against principalities, against powers, against the rulers of darkness of this world, against spiritual wickedness in high places (Ephesians 6:12)*. I had no means to fight this battle. I wasn't equipped spiritually to fight it (or so I believed). I thank God for my mother because when I couldn't pray for myself, she was interceding on my behalf. *The effectual fervent prayer of the righteous man availeth much* (James 5:16)!

One thing we MUST understand as children of God is that we are more SPIRIT than what we think. When He blew His breath or His spirit *(Ruach)* into man when creating him, Man became even MORE like Him. Your flesh merely holds the spiritual giant that you are. We were created in His image. We have the essence of the Creator; of the Almighty in our bodies so we are able to do what no other creature created can do.

The Bible says that we are more than conquerors. Greater is HE that is in me than HE that is in the world. What we must come to realize is that His strength is made perfect in our weakness. It's okay to recognize our weak moments.

You have to understand the authority that you have as a believer and as a child of the God. You have the keys to the Kingdom of Heaven. You have a seat in heavenly places. You have the ability to speak things that be not as though they are, and watch them come to fruition. We are nor powerless against the enemy. Satan has no power-compared to the Almighty one- The Lion of Judah. Walk in your authority.

[29]

The bible says He gives POWER to the faint (Isaiah 40:9) When we feel weary, that is when we should seek Him the more. I don't care where you are or if you have reached a dead end or a cycle, God is able to deliver you. He is able to save you right where you are. He is your DELIVERER!!!

Regardless of what you were connected to and what kind of lifestyle you were in, God can take those desires away and clean you up so that you don't look like what you came out of! He will take the struggle away and remove any residue of ungodly desires from your life. I am a witness that what you struggled with before, you don't have to struggle with anymore!!

Soon after the start of that dead-end relationship I began to think of ways to get out of it. In 1995, all of my high school buddies were graduating. Even though I dropped out of high school, I wanted to graduate as well. So I bought a GED preparation book. I studied hard for a month and I took the test. I scored so well that no college or university could refuse me because I had a GED. My scores allowed me to go to any university of my choosing. Once I completed that goal, I knew I was ready to leave Connecticut. My mother and my younger brother had left months before and moved to upstate New York.

Although my immediate family left, my momma's sister stayed behind. She would often call me and pray with me on the telephone. She wouldn't ask any questions about how I was living but she called me and prayed for me. I'm sure she knew how I was living, but she never judged me. I remember being thankful that she never asked because then I would never have to tell…

One day after having struggled in my mind I made a decision and I called my mother to tell her that I was coming to New York. Her response was what I needed to secure my decision. Her response was what helped me to realize that she did not give up on me and that she was praying for me. She was excited as she told the other women in the church that I was coming home, tears streaked down my face. I wanted... no I needed this battle with this particular spirit to be OVER. Home was not a particular city but home was with my momma and my brother. I going back home!

My decision to leave Connecticut was not easily accepted by the woman I was in the relationship with. She was adamant about me staying with her and I was adamant about leaving. Eventually, my stubbornness along with the will and plan of God for my life won and I was soon on a bus to NY.

When I arrived in NY, I was welcomed into my mother's house. I was glad to be back where I belonged. My mother and my relationship began to change gradually. My original plan was to go to NY and work. I was going to save enough money and go away to school.

I planned on going to Johnson and Wales University in Providence Rhode Island. That was indeed MY plan. Plans don't always go according to what we desire for ourselves. God has the final say-always...

I began working at the nearest Subway which was located in a gas station in the hood. I think that I had a homing device on me somewhere because it seemed that many men came into the store just to talk with me. It was like I was fresh meat. They knew I was not from the area. They could probably sense my insecurities; sense my issues.

I am convinced that some people are attracted to issues. These type people can sniff out someone that is vulnerable and insecure. I went on several dates until one day while working, I met a man whose smile lit up the room. I was immediately drawn to him. He would come in and talk with me while he ordered his sandwich. He would make me laugh at the simplest things. Through our conversation I learned that his family knew my family very well. Eventually, I called the number he gave me and soon after that we started dating.

One thing that I could appreciate about this man was his honesty with me. He never sold me a dream or told me things I just wanted to hear. We were friends before the relationship began. We would talk to wee hours of the morning and spend as much time as we could together. He wined and dined me.

He took me shopping and flooded my closet with new clothing and shoes. When I asked him what he did for a living, he told me the truth- that he was a drug dealer and that he knew the life he was in had consequences. He told me that whenever the police came for him they would put him away for a very long time.

When he finished explaining to me about all the consequences that came with his lifestyle he gave me a choice. He provided me with all that information and then told me that I could stay with him. I could live better than I ever had and risk going to jail one day, or if I couldn't handle his lifestyle I had every right to walk away. What do you think I chose? Instead of keeping him as a friend- and instead of keeping our relationship strictly platonic, I made the choice to stay with him.

By that time I was head over heels in love. I thought him to be the best thing that ever happened to me. In my head, I believed that this was the man I was destined to spend the rest of my

[32]

life with. I believed him to be the last man I would ever be with. So instead of listening to caution I chose to stay.

I eventually moved out of my mother's house and into his. We went everywhere together. I stopped working at Subway and spent as much time with him as I could. There really wasn't a need to work. He provided everything I needed and everything that I wanted.

I had closets full of clothes and shoes-jewels that glistened on my neck, fingers and ears, and exclusive purses. I had everything that most women my age dreamt of having. He taught me how to drive and as soon as I learned he went out and bought me a car. I had it all. And for the first time in my life I felt that I was in a wonderful place.

I was even trying to get pregnant. We both wanted children and since we planned on being together forever, we decided to have a child. In 1996, he proposed to me by dropping on his knee in the rain. I remembered thinking that life couldn't get any better than this. I hadn't been to church in months and I was not thinking about going. It was his and my world- OUR world... And I was enjoying every minute of it. I thought that he was it for me. I didn't want any other but him.

With his prompting, I enrolled at a local college and also began to work. One thing that he ensured was that I had my own money. He taught me to make sure I had my own so that I never had to rely on anyone else including him. So although he paid all the bills in our house, I was able to bank all the money I made. Later, I would find use for this money.

The lifestyle that we lived was costly. Throughout our years together there were certain incidents that caused my eyes to open to what I really was involved in. He was not a very flashy man. Meaning you couldn't tell by just looking at him on the surface that he was getting money. However, one with an eye for fashion would notice that his shirts were Versace. His tee-shirts were Ralph Lauren, Moschino and or Tommy Hilfiger. He wore clothes that most people around him hadn't been privileged to wear. He was fresh every day and he wore very expensive jewelry. Getting his jewelry pieces specifically designed by jewelers in NY City.

One night while out playing darts and checking on those who ran his drugs, he was robbed at gun point for his favorite piece of Jewelry-his Jesus piece. It's ironic now that this particular piece of jewelry was taken and was the precipice of many events that had my world come crashing all around me. Another event I can recall is when one of his soldiers got cut up in his car while he was taking care of business. He was attacked while just sitting there-in his car. There was so much blood.

I remember seeing it pooling in the seats. There were spots of blood all over the windows and the dash board. Although there was always danger and violence around us, this was the first time I saw it up close. Other things began to happen. Packages began to go missing. I knew how he was concerning money. He did not play when it came to his money. There was the constant fear of retaliation. I knew that when he retaliated it was going to be bad and it would set off a domino effect of violence and disturbing events. I was afraid for him and for me!

Due to rumors about him being in other relationships, his controlling nature, my disgusting attitude and the wear and tear of the lifestyle we were living, our relationship was tumultuous at times. When we fought, we fought hard and when we loved, we loved harder. However in the beginning of the year 1998, we both have had enough. We called off our engagement and I moved out of his house. He continued to pay my bills and for the lifestyle that I'd grown accustomed to.

With all this going on in my life, my mother had some excitement as well. She had met a gentleman and was engaged to be married. My momma and her beau married in 1998. I was very happy for her. He was a Christian as well and he had two little kids of his own. I was excited about their union and the blending of our families. I wanted another chance to be a big sister. I remember feeling nostalgic as I watched him interact with his kids. I hoped that perhaps he would be a father to me too. I wasn't looking for a replacement of Daddy because no one can replace him. However, I was looking for a male father figure that would love me and be there for me. I hoped that I would have that with my new step-dad.

In May of 1998, my boyfriend and I decided to go visit my family in Connecticut in an effort to rekindle our relationship. We thoroughly enjoyed ourselves and when we came back to NY I began to spend more time with him at his house. We had made up our minds to be together and work out the kinks in our relationship.

July 1998, would be a month I would never forget. We made plans to go to NYC to do some shopping and to get my hair done. I knew that he was also going to see his connect and send his worker back on the train with his package. The night before we left, he was downstairs in his living room counting stacks and stacks of cash. Now I have seen some cash before. I have helped him count endless stacks of cash before, but this time was different. Never in my life did I see so much money. I knew that he was getting ready to buy a huge quantity of cocaine.

We drove to NYC the following morning. He dropped me off at the hair salon and he went to handle his business. Of course, I knew what he was doing but I had no contact with his business. I never touched his drugs neither did I ever see the people who he distributed to or bought from. When He was done, he put his worker on the train and came back to meet me. We shopped and enjoyed the sights before going back home. That was the last time I was in New York City until 2014.

On July 7, 1998 I went to work from his house as usual. The only difference was that on this day I took his car which had very dark tint on the windows. It seemed to be a regular day. That is--until I ended my work day and went back to his house. As I was sitting in my car I received a text from my mother on my pager. As I went to call her back, I looked up and saw a man wearing a ski mask with a huge gun. I sat there for a moment, paralyzed and not knowing what to do.

I was thinking that we were being robbed and maybe if I rolled down the window a bit they would see it was only me and let me continue to ride past them. I knew that my life was going to change. I don't know how I knew it but I knew that whatever happened next was going to change my life forever.

I started to drive past but as I got closer to the house, I saw there were men in masks with vests on that said "DEA". I can remember feeling relieved! I was glad it was no one trying to rob us and trying to hurt me. I remembered thinking that it was going to be okay because he never kept anything where he slept at.

He always told me that. It was his mantra "Never keep your drugs where you rest your head at!" I figured the most they would find is money and probably paraphernalia. I also figured if there was something in there, it wouldn't matter because I've never sold or touched a drug in my life. They would have had to know that. Boy was I wrong!

They made me stop the car and get down on the ground. There were about ten men with huge guns drawn and pointing in my face. They threw me on the ground. I was handcuffed as they took the keys out of the ignition and proceeded to enter our house. They kept me outside as they searched the house and called a female officer. I remember wondering where my boyfriend was. I recall being so scared my stomach was turning. My teeth were chattering. I remember saying to myself that it would be okay.

I was brought in the house and there were drugs that was found. He had been cooking the cocaine in the house. There were all kinds of paraphernalia such as scales and small baggies. There was crack cocaine in the rice that I used to cook with. The DEA uncovered everything that was in that house. They searched every nook and cranny. I watched as they tore open the furniture. I watched as they cracked the code on his safe and took the jewelry we kept locked up.

They took the cash he had locked up. I watched as some put the jewelry in their pockets not even trying to hide that they were stealing from me in my home. They searched under the bed. I sat there violated as they searched my lingerie drawer and found the gun that I had recently put there. From listening to the officers, I was able to conclude that they raided his spots as well as his mother's house. His older sister was in custody as well, but he was still on the move. They had no idea where he was. One of the officers asked me to call him and lure him to the house.

How was I going to do that? He was too smart. I didn't want to lure my boyfriend. A part of me didn't want him to come back to the house. I wanted him to run. If he was free, then I knew he would take care of me. I thought about refusing to do it. Then my mind went back to when we first met and he told me that eventually these same people would come for him and he knew he would be gone for a long time. I was not prepared to go to prison but he knew his chances from the moment he started selling drugs. So I made my decision- I would call him. And what he would do would be totally up to him. I knew he would make the decision for us both.

Whether or not he came to that house was going to be totally up to him. By this time, I knew that he knew what was going on. He knew he had been hit on all sides and that the same people who raided his other spots were at his home.

As I waited to make the call, the female officer began to harass me. She told me that he had left me and was long gone by now. He had left me to take the wrap for the drugs. She told me that I was never going to get out of jail with the amount of drugs and money that they found in the house. She told me that they were well aware of his intelligence and they knew he was not coming back for me. The officer told me that they had watched him for a year but they could never get anything on him. However, this time a close affiliate ratted him out and he was going down.

She played on my insecurities. But what she didn't know was that with all the intelligence that he had, it meant nothing compared to love that he had for me. He would not leave me. He would not allow me to go down like this. I knew it with a surety. If he came to the house it was because he had a plan. If he did not come to the house it was because he had a plan-a plan for both of us. I dialed his number holding my breath waiting for him to answer the phone. When he answered the cell, it was confirmed that he knew the police were there. I didn't say too much, as a matter of fact I don't think I said anything really. I was crying,-sobbing because I knew what was going to happen. I cried because I knew that when he walked through that door, he was not going to walk out a free man. He told me he was on his way. In less than fifteen minutes he was at the door.

The rest of the night was a whirlwind. As soon as he walked in the house the DEA had guns in his face. They threw him down on the ground asking him if he had any weapons. He was telling them that he did not have anything but they were still very aggressive. When they sat him up he looked over at me and mouthed that he loved me and that it was going to be okay. But it would not be okay. Not for a long time after. My lover, my friend, my confidante, was going to prison as he predicted he would.

He and I were escorted to the police station in different vehicles. Once I got to the station, I was questioned over and over again by different cops. They played bad cop good cop in hopes that my story would change. It didn't change because I truly didn't know the answers to their questions. You would think that they would know that since they had him under investigation for over a year!

After the interrogation they handed me over to a different female correctional officer. She took me to get fingerprinted. Then she watched me as I stripped down to my underwear. I was not allowed to keep my bra because of the underwire. I was given an ugly orange jumpsuit and blue skippies.

All my jewelry was bagged up and taken away from me. I couldn't believe this was happening to me. I could not believe that I was in jail and according to the police I would be going to prison for up to fifteen years. This was crazy. My fairytale life was over. What was I going to do now?

The next day, I woke up in my jail cell. It was very small. The actual cell was in a pod with other cells. So although I had my own cell, there were other females in my pod. I woke up nauseated and feeling so heavy. My head was throbbing- and my eyes were swollen from all the crying I had done. I knew my life was over. I knew my life with him was over. I started to throw up bile. That made my headache worse. I remember wondering if my mother knew what was going on. I remember feeling ashamed because yet again I had let her down. I let myself down. I didn't know that our arrest had made the local news. I didn't know that it also made the local newspaper. When I got my phone call, I did call my mother to see about getting out. There was nothing she could do because she didn't have the money nor did she have collateral to get me out. This was such a hopeless situation I thought.

Later that day, I found myself talking to God. Funny how every time I found myself in trouble, I would begin to pray. He was indeed- a very present help in the time of trouble! I found myself asking him to forgive me for the bad choices I'd made. I knew I was not a victim.

Never had I even thought that I was one. I made a decision to stay with him. I made a decision even when he told me what I was getting into. While waiting to see what my fate held, I had several anxiety attacks in which my heart would beat so hard, feeling like it was beating out of my chest. I would sweat profusely.

I couldn't catch my breath at times. I just knew I was going to die and perhaps I welcomed death. What was life without my boyfriend anyways? But as I cried a feeling of peace enveloped me. It surrounded me as I quietly sobbed.

Soon I stopped the crying and laid there with my eyes wide open. I was trying to figure out what was exactly happening right then. What was this I was feeling? It was a feeling that I never felt before. This peace that I suddenly felt helped me to fall asleep. And I slept for hours.

A few days later I saw my boyfriend at our felony hearing. He stared at me and mouthed how sorry he was. He was asking me if I was okay. He was so concerned about me that I didn't understand why he would be. He was the one they were depicting as a monster. The one who had sold drugs to his community and to his peers. It wouldn't be until after the hearing that I realized just how much drugs was in that house.

I didn't want to look at him but I could not turn a way. I wanted to remember everything I could about him. In my mind I had already forgiven him but my heart was devastated because I knew I would be raising our child by myself.

Yes, I knew I was pregnant. I just had this feeling after four years of trying to get pregnant. I remembered how I felt when I was pregnant before and it was the exact same feeling-constantly throwing up; and always feeling fatigued. Yup, I was pregnant alright. After all those years of hoping for a baby with this man, we had finally succeeded only to have our dream of being a family turned into a living nightmare...

My mother hired an attorney for me with the money my boyfriend was able to get to her. This attorney was not in my favor at all. It wasn't until I met with him that I realized I was really in a dire situation and it didn't matter that I never touched or sold drugs in my life. He asked me what my dream career was. I told him that I wanted to be a teacher. Well, he told me that I could now give that dream up because I would never teach.

He told me that the district attorney was offering me fifteen years and he was not budging. My lawyer told me to prepare for the worst because this was a year of political opportunities. He said they were going to use my case to make a statement to other women in the area. My family knew nothing about the legal system and I continued believing that I would come away from this unscathed, I was so wrong!

I can recall my time in jail like it was yesterday. My girlfriends came to visit me, just to cheer me up. But when they left, all I would do was cry. The only thing I knew how to do at this point was pray. I prayed to my Father to get me out of this situation. I promised Him that I would not be in another situation like this. I couldn't eat or sleep. I refused to go out for recreation. Sooner than later, my paternal aunt and her boyfriend as well my paternal grandmother posted bail.

I was so thankful to them for coming to rescue me. I am still very grateful because they did not have to pay that money. My grandmother did not have to put up her house. I hate to think about what would have happened if they did not do so. No one else stepped up to help me- not one other person. For that I am FOREVER grateful.

My family bailed me out and I was free-or so I thought. My boyfriend was never released. As a matter of fact, he wouldn't see the outside of a prison's walls for many, many years to come. His original charge was an A-1 felony which is equivalent to murder because of the amount of drugs and money that were in the house. In the end, the DEA seized the cars, motorcycles, computers, jewelry, money and anything of value that was in the house.

When I got out of jail, I remember feeling like the world was going to swallow me up. This man had basically been everything to me and I wasn't quite sure how I was going to survive. I recall asking my girl-friends one day while sitting on my grandmother's porch "What am I going to do now?!" My friends were never known to sugar coat anything. We told each other the truth about ourselves, whether the other liked it or not.

One of my friends responded "You are going to live!" Those words and their support gave me life in one of the darkest moments in my existence. I also remembered some of the things my boyfriend would say to me "*Ke, Get that money! So you don't have to depend on nobody! Aint nobody going to give you anything. Save what you can because there will be day when you are going to need it.*" And he was so right! And So I prepared myself for that journey... learning how to be a mother to this child. ...

My final court date was in 1999. I was told by my lawyer up until the day we went in to stand before the judge that all I would get was five years' probation. I was told that all I had to do was agree with whatever the judge said. As I stood in front of that judge and he read to me a list of things that I had to agree to doing, tears flowed out of my eyes. I put my hand on the Bible and agreed with the judge that I was in cohorts with selling, and packaging crack/cocaine.

I guess I was in cohorts since I benefitted from the sales of the drugs right? There I was pregnant and totally confused about how the legal system worked. I was a product of "*association*" and the fact that I benefitted from the drugs sold-it was my crime.

Let's just say that I did not leave that court with what I was promised by my lawyer. I literally stood in that court room, pregnant and crying thinking that all my dreams for my life were over. Who would hire a felon? How would I finish college? How would I drive since New York State suspends convicted felons licenses for a short season? Life as I knew it, the glamour and the glitz was over. Now reality set in and I had to think about how I was going to live for my son. How was I going to create a viable life for my baby boy?

I eventually moved out of the studio apartment I was living in and moved into the projects in order to take care of myself and my newborn. My prince was born in February 1999. It was an amazing experience. I can remember reminding myself that I was a mother now and I had someone to live for. He was beautiful and healthy. He was all I could ask for and more. He had little freckles on his nose that I would kiss as he slept in my arms. And he looked just like his father.

[43]

Even though I was totally in love with my son, depression set in after his birth. Women that are prone to depression are more likely to experience postpartum depression after child birth. I didn't tell anyone what I was going through, but if someone were to look closely they would see the signs of the illness.

I did manage to stay in school but my grades were suffering badly due to my brand new responsibility. One day I went to sit with my counselor to discuss my grades. The man who once told me I could accomplish anything was now so cold to me. I couldn't figure out why. I was going to ask him why but I never got the chance to ask.

When he went up to make a copy of something in my folder, I got a glimpse of a newspaper clipping. So when he left his office, I looked into my file and there, clipped to the inside of the manila folder, was the newspaper article discussing the arrest of my boyfriend and me. I was horrified. Needless to say, I understood why his conversation with me had changed. He no longer believed in me. And I no longer believed in myself.

It is a sad thing to be so concerned about what people think of you. People cannot determine your future. Only you can. When you give people enough power over you that they begin to validate who you are, you have given them more power than you yourself have. Remember, where you are now is not your final destination!

I dropped out of school, feeling as if my lifetime goals were unobtainable. I met several notable people during my days at school, but that wasn't enough to keep me faithfully attending. There was one female that attended school with me who would call me, and encourage me not to give up. She would eventually graduate and move away from Utica, but I would see her again and it wouldn't be on good terms.

Life didn't stop. I went out clubbing, I drank, I went to work, and I took care of my son to the best of my ability. It was just a mundane cycle. I firmly believe that when you are not fulfilling your purpose in life, it will become a never ending cycle. You have an assignment on this earth. There are plans that have been designed for you before you were created in your mother's womb. You have to fulfill that assignment.

I often brought my son to see his dad while he was still in the county jail. He couldn't hold him but he could kiss him. I would see the wonder in his eyes. I could see the love he had for his boy. It was there for all to see. He would arrange for his son to be taken care of while he was away in prison. His family was always a help to me. They would call for my baby and come to get him to give me a break. His friends rose to the challenge of helping me with my son.

Anything that my baby needed all I had to do was ask and he would have it. But I was learning how to be independent so there were very few times that I asked. They never stopped providing. How appreciative I am to his family and his few true friends. I am so appreciative of my family and friends that *did* what they could to help me. Because of them, I was able to get through one of the most difficult times in my life.

I frequented church often. However, I was not always comfortable there. I remember when I was pregnant with my son; there were always messages about teenage pregnancy and pregnancy before marriage. I would sit there and try not to let the tears that were building up inside me cascade down my cheeks.
I'm thinking *"we're family!"* Surely you are supposed to address the sin but why the need for constant rebuke about being pregnant.

Even after my son's birth it was often preached about. Granted, there were two other young ladies that were pregnant

[45]

or parenting as well but I am sure they felt the same way I did. Now I understand preaching holiness, but what I don't understand is beating up on people that are already feeling guilty about what they have done. This was what I felt was happening. I was being beaten up because I chose to have my baby. This is something that takes place in the body of Christ often. Ministers use the sacred desk to be condescending to their parishioners.

Proclaiming the Word of God is our duty but it is not our duty to beat up on God's people. Everything we do we must do in love. We can be passionate about the cause of Christ and holy living but we must continue to show love. We know that love is not a feeling but an action word. Even in those sermons, I should've been able to feel God's love. The Bible states that **_He chastens whom he loves_** *(*Proverbs 3:12) I felt NO love in those messages. I felt NO love in the sermons preached. I felt condemnation and I am sure the other women felt it the same.

No one from the church was concerned about how I was doing or at least they never asked me how I was doing. There I was, battling major depressive episodes and no one knew or cared enough to help me through it. I don't even know what I expected from them. I knew I expected something because half of them in attendance were family.

There were few people who helped me during this time and that was my mother, my nana, and my aunt and uncle. I began to have some resentment in my heart. It's a dangerous place to be sitting in God's temple with anger and other issues in your heart against the man or woman of God. I knew this so eventually I stopped going.
I just didn't want to be at a place where I felt bad all the time. To me it was not a safe place. I was already feeling bad. Why would I go somewhere every Sunday just to feel worse?

[46]

Believe it or not, there are so many people who are just turned off from going to church services. Church hurt is real and many people have experienced it during their lifetime. Why do you think that the television ministry has bloomed? Folk would rather sit at home and send their monies to a tele-evangelist than go to their local church. How sad is that? No one wants to be beat up. Yes sin is wrong (no question) but show me how to get out of it. Teach me how to live my life sinless!

Teach me the practicality of living life but living holy! There's a song that says "I've learned how to live holy, I learned how to live right!" Living holy is a learned behavior. We have to be taught how to abstain. We have to be taught what God expects from us. God's holy is not our holy! **TEACH AND REACH**. Love and correct. This is what the Church should be doing! And when people mess up, they should know that when they go to church they are in the right place to receive God's forgiveness. They should know that someone is there that can help them through their issue-with no judgement.

As much as I had distaste for the church, I still felt like I should be there. My nana would often encourage me to attend services. Reminding me that it was best for me and my child to be in church. My nana often voiced many regrets to me and one thing that she regretted that she didn't attend church with her children while they were young. She sent them to church at times, but she stopped going. Nana would encourage me to do what was right in the sight of the Lord.

Whenever I didn't have answers to my questions she would say "I can tell you but pray about it first!" And so I knew that prayer was important in my family. I later came to realize that intercession was a mantle passed down through the generations and it would rest heavily on me.
My mother taught my brother and me to pray. We would be praying with her and she would ask us to pray as well. I would

pray for my Barbie dolls and my brother his GI Joe men, but prayer was essential and it has been prayer that pulled me through some major circumstances.

While trying to come to terms with my life I had made some strides. I had obtained my first car. It was a 95' Dodge Neon-green. I was coming along-managing my depression. I still wasn't going to church though. I didn't want to be reminded that my dreams were now deferred. I didn't want to be reminded of the fact that I had made a mess out of my life and it was plain to see by everyone that noticed me.

In 2000, I began working at a local call center for a cellular service. This was an easy job and a lot of people from the neighborhood worked there. I wasn't seeing anyone in particular but I was being actively pursued. I didn't think I was ready for any relationship. My son's father was locked up, and I was trying to live, work and give my son some semblance of a life. They had given him life on the end of his sentence but I wanted to do right by him. So I really tried to just stay away from men. I just wanted to work and take care of my son.

One of my suitors was a young man that was a few years younger than me. We worked together at the call center and we developed a friendship. I remember him having flowers sent to my desk on a few occasions. I was not really interested in him as he was not my type. I prefer dark-skinned men that were at least my height or taller. He was none of those things. But he was a good listener. He would listen to me ramble on about life. He showed genuine interest in me. Sooner than later we became inseparable. Although I had no plans to be with this man, his charisma soon won me over.

We would go out for dinner and movies. We had fun with one another and seemingly enjoyed each other's company. We were always together. He met my son and eventually moved into the apartment with us. I fell in love with this man who appeared to adore me and my son. He made me laugh-he was very personable. Everyone he met loved him. His personality was contagious and people all over the city knew him-especially the women.

I thought well just maybe this is my happily ever after. Isn't that ludicrous? One year ago I was in another relationship thinking that it was the ONE! Now I was in another thinking the same thing. Sometimes women can be so delusional! We may want something so bad that we just continue to put ourselves in situations that are not good for us. I had no business jumping into another relationship so soon! But who was going to CHECK ME?? No one was interested in my love life.

Those that I would listen to were doing the same thing. It is so sad to say that it is the NORM for some women AND some MEN to jump in relationship after relationship. This is our society. Promiscuity seems to be the way of life. It seems like very few people want to be in committed relationships anymore.

I hurt my son's father by being dishonest. He always told me to tell him the truth when it came down to my decisions about our relationship. I did not do that. He had to find out through the streets. That is a regret that I have always had. However, I am so glad that he and I are very good friends to this day and we co-parent our child together along with his wife and my husband.

I fell in love with the things that I thought I always wanted. He did not have a lot of money but he made me feel like I was the only one for him. He gave me something that money cannot buy. This was lacking in the previous relationship. Money made our world go around and I was reminded whose money it was. But he affirmed me with his show of affection and by what I thought was a genuine display of emotion for my son and me.

The good times that we had prior to him moving in, would not last too much longer. We began to have arguments and those arguments began to evolve into physical altercations. Either he would hit me or I would hit him first. It didn't matter. I wasn't going to allow anyone to put their hands on me and he wasn't going to allow it either. The relationship quickly became toxic.

We fought over the silliest stuff but then we fought over life and death. When your significant other begins another relationship and is intimate with that person, they are now putting you at risk for diseases that can cause death.

We fought about all the different women he was sleeping with. They would call my house and tell me exactly where he was. He had these women around his family and around his friends. Nothing was sacred to him. Places and people that I thought were sacred were not off limits to him. They would tell me how he was spending money on them. And since he had lost his job, he was spending MY money on them! We fought over the hours in the club he was spending and the times he would come home high.

He would drive them in the car that I bought. We fought over his need to look fly in the latest gear but could care less about what I was wearing. I wasn't trying to wear the latest fashion but I was trying to take care of our house.

We even fought about his obsession with gambling. He would take whatever money he could get his hands on and head to the casino. Sometimes he lost and sometimes he won. But it was a gamble and he felt we didn't have anything to lose. I loved him hard but he fought me harder. Before I knew it I was pregnant with my second son.

My lifestyle changed when I learned I was pregnant with my son. I stopped going out but he kept on. He lived for the night life it seemed. He would come home high off life and drunk off alcohol. He got a job then he lost it after a while. Our household to take a financial hit. He would take my car out and stay out all night coming home in the wee hours of the morning. The rumors didn't stop about the women. It seemed that everyone knew that he was cheating on me. The fights got worse.

One evening, we were fighting so badly about his alleged affairs. I remember feeling so hopeless and desperate. Along with the physical abuse came the emotional and verbal abuse. He would often tell me how no one was going to want me. He would tell me how I was fat and for long periods of time he would stop sleeping with me.
This was huge to me because the intimacy was something that we both loved-the closeness. That was how we got it right.

We used to argue and then we would make love. Isn't that how it goes ladies? Break up to make up? How silly we can be to think that having sex would alleviate our issues in our relationships. He stopped doing all those things that I felt I needed-those things which validated and affirmed me. No more sweet words or touches. Gone were those days where love was what I felt. Gone were the days of romancing me.

Our fighting eventually became public because of the scars we wore and because I would call his mother or his father to ask them for help or to ask them if they'd seen him with my car. I remember his mother and I having a conversation about him. She asked me if this was what I wanted for my life. Of course, I told her no. that I wanted much more for my children. She asked me if I had considered having an abortion. I politely told her NO! I was having my baby. I was never going to kill another child. I learned from my first mistake. There was no other option. I was having my baby. I remained in that relationship. It never got better. We would try and it would appear to be getting better but in actuality it got worse.

In March 2001, we had an altercation that left me at the bottom of a flight of stairs. Soon after that fight, I was admitted into labor and delivery because my son was coming 4 months early.

The birth of my son was a scary situation for me. I was so afraid for my baby. I was also afraid for myself. I knew that if I lost my baby, it would take a miracle for me to bounce back. The doctors at the local hospital thought he would not make it. They basically told me to prepare for him to die.

I was not trying to hear that. They sent me to a neonatal intensive care unit in a neighboring city. My boyfriend was there with me except when he left to go check on my oldest son. In spite of what was going on with us, he always remained loving towards my child. Because the doctors wanted to keep the baby inside of me longer, I was on total bed rest.

I was kept in bed with my head down and my feet up. We were hoping that the baby would stay in as long as possible. This worked for one week. I started spotting soon after and my doctor determined that my son was breech and his heart rate had started to drop. It was time for an immediate emergency cesarean.

I was whisked out of the hospital room and prepped for surgery. The attending doctor was a gentle man who talked to me and tried to calm me down even after the anesthesiologist worked. My boyfriend was there with me. He held my hand as the operating assistants put up this blue blocker that acted as a shield from me seeing what was going on.

The doctor and his assistants worked together whispering as they went along. Tears seeped through the corners of my lids as I thought about what was happening. My boyfriend kept peeking over the blue barrier, hoping to get a look at his namesake. Soon after the surgery began it was done. I heard not one peep from my new son. He didn't cry or make a peep. However, from the emotion that my boyfriend was displaying, I knew that something was not right. As fast as he came into this world, was as fast as he was taken from me. I never got to see my child until the next morning. By the time I saw him he was in an incubator with tubes going into his nose and other parts of his body.

During my stay in the hospital I was hoping that my child's father and I would rekindle what we once had. The easiness that made our relationship work, I wanted back. He came back every day after our child was born spending hours in the N.I.C.U. We couldn't hold our son because he was so tiny. He was born 1lb 10.5 oz. and could fit in the palm of my hand, he was so small. The doctors were crossing their fingers for him. They were unsure if he was going to make even now that he was born. He was not out of harm's way as of yet. They were feeding him through tubes as well.

The nurses had tapped so many of his veins that they eventually went to his head to give him antibiotics for an infection that he contracted. My son was having such a hard time with just trying to survive. I thought "How unfair is this for him. He has done nothing to deserve any of this." Yet, here he was fighting to live in a world that would be cruel to him.

My ordeal was not over yet. I came down with a fever from an infection that I had contracted. The on-call doctor that was attending to me came into my room one morning on rounds and pressed on my still sore cesarean wound. He determined that the infection was in my belly. He asked for an assistant to come in with certain supplies and before I knew it he popped my staples out of my belly and stretched open my wound. He poured antiseptic into my belly to clean and disinfect. I was in extreme pain.

I had no time for medication, nor a warning that he was going to do this. I cried out at the pain I was feeling. When he left, the nurse apologized profusely for his bedside manner. She gave me some pain medicine and allowed it to work before she started to dress my wound. I would have to let my caesarean heal from the inside out with no staples after his *"procedure."*

I was discharged from the hospital before my son had even stabilized. Leaving my son in that hospital was one of the hardest things I had ever done at that time. However he was just not ready to come home. How helpless I felt. How guilty I felt. I asked myself what kind of mother was I that I couldn't even protect my child! I felt like I failed him. I failed my son. He didn't ask to be born and yet here he was born early and fighting for his life. No help from me or his daddy, fighting on his own.

One night the doctor on call called my home and told me that my son had another "episode" during which he stopped breathing. The doctor asked me what I wanted to do. He asked me when I would be ready to take him off the ventilator. I told that doctor that as long as my son fought to live then it is his job to do his best to make that happen. The next day, my mother and my aunt took me to the hospital to see my baby. Only two people were allowed at a time. So the two of them went in and they came back out about twenty minutes later.

When I went in to see my baby he was so oily from the anointed oil that my mother and my aunt used to anoint him with. I can recall the nurses asking me "*What were they doing?!*" I told her that they were praying for my child. When my baby finally left the hospital, he never returned. Since his birth he has NEVER been a sickly child. That's the power of prayer!

My baby had so many issues that he had to overcome. He had to learn how to suck a bottle, and since he couldn't do that on his own, I had to feed him with a special bottle called the Haberman feeder. This bottle helped me to squeeze small amounts into the corner of his mouth so that he could then swallow the milk. After his stay in the hospital, his father and I had drifted apart--again. There were so many fights and so many women.

I was quickly becoming a person that I recognized from my youth. I knew exactly who this broken woman was that was always on edge; always crying. I had become depressed more than ever. I wouldn't discuss my situation with anyone fearing that no one would understand my reasons to stay with this man. I really stopped caring about myself. He consumed my world. I was so wrapped up into him that I couldn't see the situation for what it was. His cheating made me think that something was wrong with me.

I started analyzing myself again. *I'm too fat. I'm too dark. My lips are too thick. No one sees me. No one loves me. No one will ever love me. I'm ruined. I'm washed up. Who am I without him?* I was pathetic!

It was happening all over again. The self-hate... See how the enemy preys on what you already think about yourself or your situation? He doesn't use new tactics. He uses the same ones! He began to influence the negative image that I already had of myself. I had already lost the person I was when I allowed him to come back the first time he hit me or the first time he cheated. But I couldn't just blame him. He didn't just hit me out of the blue; we fought! So I felt guilty as well.

Let's pause right here. Ladies, we should never think it is okay to put our hands on a man. If he ever was to retaliate and put his hands on us then we would be the first to call the cops. There are men who suffer from domestic violence as well.

There are men who are verbally abused, emotionally abused and financially abused by their partners. There are some women who are so power hungry that they emasculate their men. They want their partners to depend solely on them. Domestic abuse towards men happens more than we think. Many of us have this predisposed idea that women are the only ones being abused, that is just not so.

Some women abuse their men with the words that they say (verbal abuse) - the words that they use to manipulate them into doing what they want them to do. It has never been God's intention that woman rule over men. If you look closely at the body of Christ, you can see this epidemic of emasculated men. You may see some women pastors, or apostles (women in higher positions of authority in church) have a hard time submitting at home. If you look closely, you will see that her husband is bitter and has resentment towards her and the church. This is a form of abuse and it needs to stop!

During this time in my relationship, I was unrecognizable to MYSELF. I lost my morals and my substance. I lost the proud black woman that my mother raised me to be. My mom raised me never to take a beating from a man- never to allow anyone to just dog you out. She raised me to take pride in myself. That girl was gone-and in her place was this female who depended on this man to love her when he didn't even know what love was. I didn't even know how to love myself. So how then, could I help myself in this situation? Where could I get strength from?

Sometimes I sit back and I think about this time in my life. I think about how much I loved that man. I think about all the things we been through and how I could not leave him alone. It was like my soul was deeply entangled with his and indeed it was. I felt that if this man was not in my life then life wasn't worth living.

Through all the pain we went through, all the pain that we caused each other, I just couldn't let go. I loved him so much that I loved him more than I loved myself. What a dangerous situation!! It took years after the demise of this relationship to get over my feelings, the trauma that I endured and everything else that was baggage.

To this day, I don't understand why I loved him so much. I didn't know why it took almost nine years for us to separate when the relationship was toxic from the start. There were soul ties. I was so deeply entangled with him-emotionally, physically, and even spiritually. But thanks be unto God that eventually I recognized the situation for what it was- better yet, I came to grips with the person I was!!

Before my son came home from the hospital, my boyfriend left me. That was my first break down of many to come. He left me and moved in with his aunt. Of course, he was still seeing his women friends as well. Looking back now, it really was for the best. But I could not see it then. All I could see was him leaving me with a baby that had special needs. My oldest was in his terrible two's and was causing chaos as toddlers do. Luckily, his father's side of the family was good people and they cared for him as he was their own.

The newborn's family were not as friendly towards me neither was I towards them. They never offered a helping hand to me concerning my child after he was born. I guess they didn't want to deal with me so they only saw my child when his father picked him up. They didn't like me so I guess my son had to suffer for that.

I don't think that I was looking for a hand out. I knew enough to know that nothing is free. I was just looking for support and my newborn's family did not give it. It seemed as if they were just happy to see my son's dad with someone else. I suppose that wasn't all too bad. Besides the relationship was chaotic and someone was bound to get hurt. I would want to see my sons with someone that they were not always fighting with too. I don't blame them at all.

So when the baby came home, I had my friends who supported me tremendously. My child's dad did come and get him as much as I would let him. I had some of my family and I had my nana. These people were a great help to me. He was still so little.

By the time he came home he was only 3lbs. He wore preemie clothes until he was about 6 months old. Because he was so little, I was so afraid to hold him. It's sad to say that my little one did not get all the nurturing he deserved and he needed. Because of the post-partum depression I had a hard time forming a bond with my baby boy. Maybe it was because I never got the opportunity to bond with him after birth since he was whisked away.

This is the way many women who suffer from post-partum depression feel. I know now that I am not the only woman who has gone through this nor am I the last woman. I thought to myself that I was a failure. I didn't believe that I was a good mother. How could I be? I was totally lost! Women who suffer from depression are more likely to experience post-partum depression. I loved my son but I had a hard time showing him.

My girl- friends would be the ones who came to the house to nurture the baby. They would assist me as much as they could. They were such a blessing to me when I needed them the most. I didn't have to call for them, they were just there.

At present day, I look my child in his big beautiful brown eyes and all the love that I have for him comes pouring out. It took me many, many years to overcome the condemnation that was associated with me feeling as I failed my son. God forgave me and my son has too, I was able to forgive myself.

The end of 2001 was tumultuous indeed-battling with this silent disease, battling suicidal thoughts, battling with my son's father, battling with the new women in his life, battling with who I had become. I was tired of battling. I wanted to end it all. I wanted to disappear and never resurface again.

But things were looking better for me. I just couldn't see it. I had gotten a job working at a local non-profit organization. The executive director was a woman who saw my potential and under her tutelage I had begun to thrive. She knew my criminal history but gave me a chance anyways.

She eventually found out about the abusive relationship I was in but she never judged me for going back. One thing we must understand is that even when things are better than they have even been in your life, your enemy will make it seem like you are barely hanging on.

Here I was finally able to get off welfare but I couldn't see this as being a milestone. Some people base their happiness on their partners. So if their partner leaves, they are no longer happy. You should have joy from within. Let your joy come from God. Your joy should not be based on people, places or things but it should be something that you have indefinitely. Life is hard and sometimes throws us curves that we are not prepared for.

In 2002, I began to get myself together. Or shall I say the Lord began to work some things out of me? I started going back to church. I did talk about depression with some of the leaders in the church but their suggestion was prayer. Of course, prayer works but I wasn't spiritually equipped to battle the spirit of depression.

My prayers were shallow, one sided and filled with the gimmee's. Gimme this Lord or Gimme that.... I didn't have enough faith to believe that God could bring me out. I believe that we (the church) MUST become more equipped to handle the psychological issues of people who are in desperate need of help.

Mental illness is huge in our society and I don't think that most churches are prepared to handle the illness. You can't advise a babe in Christ to "pray" her way through situations in which she has no idea what to pray about. She has no idea how to pray. Prayer is something that needs to be taught. Even Jesus gave his disciples a blueprint on how to pray. Prayer is a vehicle of communication between Abba Father and ourselves.

Yes, prayer is a weapon as well. And like with any weapon, when used correctly it will defeat its opponent but used haphazardly it can be detrimental to the one wielding it. If I don't believe that God will bring me out or change my situation, why am I praying? Without faith it is impossible to please God. Prayer puts you in communication with God and allows you access to the will that he has for your life.

I had a Caucasian friend who suggested that I go to see a counselor for my depression. So I found myself seeing a counselor at her private practice. Believe it or not, she helped me. She helped me enough to see me. She helped me with really taking a look at depression and the natural side of it. I know now from all my years of research, studying and hearing the voice of God concerning mental illness that these diagnoses are only natural symptoms to a spiritual disease. One can be so fragmented in their soul and their spirits that there are natural results. I believe this is a reason why there is so much mental illness in today's society. There are spiritual undertones for mental illness.

The absence of mental illness and the presence of a healthy well-adjusted personality contributes effectively to your life. The problem is that so many people have not evolved into what therapists would say "well-adjusted." There are so many people especially women, who are *"soul sick."* This basically means that there are women all over the world that are sick in their souls-the very seat of their emotions, their intellect.

They have been fragmented in so many areas of their lives and have not either sought help or don't know where to seek help from. I know and have heard so many women testimonies or stories. These stories depict the seriousness of the matter. There are so many women that have been left feeling frazzled, disappointed, broken, desolate, exhausted, burned out, unappreciated and the list can go on.

I often wonder even now what Eve, the mother of creation, felt as she walked out of paradise into a world of which she had no knowledge. How she must have felt when her son murdered the other? How she must have wished she could retract her arm from reaching towards the forbidden fruit. Maybe she was thinking and asking herself why Adam didn't stop her from making that grave decision.

After all, he was there. He was the one God gave the declaration to. Eve's feelings and situation were real. Our feelings and situations as women are real too!! We are like Eve in so many ways. We each have made poor decisions and had to face the consequences for those decisions. We have had failures.

We have felt the guilt associated with those failures. However, it's time that we addressed them. No more hiding. No more wishing them away. No more being afraid that people are going to judge us for our past mistakes. No more being held captive by our past. No more self-sabotage because we think we don't deserve the goodness and mercy that God bestows upon us. No more condemnation. We are free in the name of Jesus Christ our Lord and King according to Romans 8:2 *"Therefore, there is now no condemnation to them which are in Christ Jesus, who walk not after the flesh, but after the spirit."*

So many Christian women are living their life in bondage. They are not free. They are not free to be themselves. They have lived to please so many people: their parents, their boyfriends, their friends etc. They cannot enjoy life because of the bondage of personal guilt and condemnation.

These women are not free to enjoy the grace of God and his love. Their personal failures and the failures of others hang over them like a black cloud. Rejection, low self-esteem, and fear hang like weights around their necks and they are enslaved to these barbells of torment.

Understand that is not God's intent for you to live your life in bondage. He wants you to be totally free. **"I am come that they might have life and that they might have it more abundantly."** (John 10:10)

This was me. I was in bondage. But God was pulling on me to get free. I believed the lies that I told myself, I believed the lie of the enemy!!! When he told me that I should just kill myself, I thought my sons would be better off with my mother. When he told me that I was to black, fat and ugly, I was thinking that I would never be thought of as pretty. I was feeling guilty about the things I had done and the decisions that I made in my life.

The years 2002-2003 went by in a blur. After the separation with my youngest child's father I was barely living. I was going about life daily but my soul was still tied to this man. I was going out to clubs hoping to see him. Often times I would see him and he was there with different women. Black women, white women, Asian women, married women it didn't matter. I was doing things that were not in my character. I was going to women's homes, fighting in the streets, going to jail for harassment etc.

It seemed like every time I looked up, I was in jail because of something crazy I had done. I was trying to get myself together but it seemed as if I was caught in a web and I just could not shake him. At times I would stay away from him and do well with ignoring my feelings. But then we slept together and it would start all over the again.

He didn't want to be with me or maybe he did. I don't know. I believe that I was a safety net for him. He was a safety net for me. I didn't want anyone else. I was programmed to think that no one else would want me anyways. He was the only man that my children knew and I wanted to keep it that way.

He was with so many women I couldn't count. However, I do recall two particular women that stand out. One of these particular women was the one I befriended in college. She ended up sleeping with him as well. Another woman he was with he really fell hard for. I knew I had lost him to her.

I recall the different arguments that we would have;-the fights in the streets. I remember one night, after he slept with me he went back home. I brought my children to a sitter's house and I followed him. I watched him pick up his woman and then I

watched as they walked in the park. I was livid. I could see the love that he had for her as he held her hand.
Of course, I interrupted them. He and I started arguing and then she interrupted the argument.

We started to fist fight. He grabbed me by my arms and held me as his girlfriend tore into me. She dug me in my face and began to scratch me leaving welts from the corner of my left eye to my cheekbone. They left me there in that park. Well, he left me there in that park. He walked away from me to go with her. I remember tears streaming down my face, the saltiness burning the new welts on my face.

After that night, I wanted in my hearts of hearts to finally be done with this man. I tried my hardest to move on. We couldn't stand one another. We were often in court for visitation and child support. Every time we saw one another it was evident that we hated each other. Well, I was trying to hate him.

During this time, I was trying to rekindle my relationship with God. I started to feel a "pull" in my spirit. I began to go to church again. I wasn't always consistent but I was going. My mother loved the fact that I was at least attending again. I felt so far from God. I was sitting in the pew and I was in a backslidden state. I was not talking to him the way I knew to- I was just going through the motions of attending church. I didn't understand that even though I was lost, I was not forgotten. God was there, waiting on me to talk to him again. I refused to. In retrospect, I believe that I was angry with God, even though I had made the bad decisions.

I was a *"church girl"* so why was I so lost? Why wasn't anyone helping me reach Him. No one cared. They were waiting on me to go up for altar call; well I wasn't ready for that. I wasn't ready to admit to God that I was the one that was wrong! He was wrong for not helping me when I needed him the most. How could he love me and call me his child when my life was so bleak? Those were questions in my head. Eventually I would slack off going to church again.

I made so many bad decisions. I remember going away to Albany and leaving my children in a hotel room with some other children-stupid decision. When I got back to my hotel, police were there waiting to question me. I was placed under arrest and my children were taken into the custody of the state.

My two children (at the time) were taken away from me and were in foster care for about a week. This was one of the most horrific times in my life. I remember having to go to court to get them back and even after I had them I still had to prove I was a fit parent. I went through the motions of doing what was expected of me and what I really wanted in my heart but there were times when I felt that perhaps they would've been better off with someone else.

In June 2004, my world spun on its axis. My nana who was my confidante, died. I will never forget that day that I was called to the hospital. We had to let her go. My heart broke into a million pieces. I thought to myself "THIS IS IT!! I cannot take it anymore!!" I could not handle it. I did not want to go to the funeral or the wake.-but I made myself go. I cried and I cried for days.

It was like being suffocated. I could not get my thoughts and my mind straight. Her death rocked my world. But on the night of her funeral, I recall sitting in my room, crying, and all of a sudden I could smell her. It was distinct, yet so loud. I could smell her perfume. My heart stopped hurting as much. I continued to cry but I knew my Nana was in a better place.

I mourned my grandmother for a very long time. I didn't know how to let go. I didn't like people to talk about her but in my thoughts she was always present. I have never gotten over the loss of my Nana but I have healed. I have learned to rebuild myself around this great loss.

It took years; it took God's healing virtue to repair my heart. This was a *defining* moment for me. It has forever shaped my concept of love. The person who knew my stuff and loved me unconditionally was gone. I had to accept that. I had to learn that she was not the only person who loved me that much-who KNEW me and loved me anyway. God did and does!

Somehow my EX and I got back together .I don't know how or know why we would even try again but we did. He was with me at the funeral. We had our second son in 2005. This child was the apple of his eye. He looked just like him. I just knew our child would make him stay. I just knew this child would save our relationship. This child would keep him home.

If I couldn't keep him, or his eldest son couldn't keep him, surely the one that was his splitting image would keep him with his family. I knew NOTHING!! I should've known better! The very day I went into labor I could not find him. He never came home the night before. I had to have his friend call him to get him to come home to take me to the hospital. I was in active labor and he was out doing what he did best. Still I stayed.

During the time that I was pregnant with my third son. I remember one night in particular I received a call from one woman that he was involved with. She told me all about their relationship and how he planned on leaving me and the kids. I confronted him about it when he finally returned home from the club.

[67]

Of course the altercation became physical. Who hit who first, I am not even sure anymore. It doesn't even matter. What I knew for sure on this day that I was in something that I could not get out of myself. My mind was too warped and thought only how I could save this relationship. I had no real thoughts of getting out!

I am praying that someone reads this book and gets help that and that they get OUT!!! Domestic violence is very real. It can end in death. There are over "4,000 deaths of women who die because of domestic violence." On an average, women would leave the domestic violence relationship 7 times before she leaves for good!! (http://www.domesticabuseshelter.org/infodomesticviolence.htm)

In late 2005, word on the streets was that my eldest son's father was coming home. The streets were buzzing with anticipation of what he was going to do when he came home. People wanted to see what was going to happen between him and I since our relationship was disrupted. Would I stay where I was or would I leave and go back to my first love in the city? There really wasn't an option for me.

I didn't feel there was an option for us to get back together again. Too much had happened since he was incarcerated. Too much had been done. There were too many rumors surrounding me and then there was this relationship I was in. I don't think that my boyfriend saw it that way.

We would argue for days about him coming home. He would start accusing me of wanting to be with him. That was the furthest from my mind. I was so lost. All I wanted was to make our relationship work. I was so delusional. There was nothing I could do to make that relationship work.

I could not change him and he could not change me. We were just not meant to be together but like everything else I had a hard time letting go! I could not let go of this man. My soul was so tied to him. It was only about him. So when he asked me to marry him, I readily said yes!

However, we talked in detail about him giving up the women, the drugs, the alcohol, and to limit his gambling and his weekend splurges in the nightclubs. We talked about him being present and being around more. We talked about the abuse and the need for it to stop. We both agreed to work on our communication. We agreed to not put hands on each other but to walk away from arguments or debates that could eventually heat up. I prayed that this would work and that he really meant what he said. I prayed that I could uphold my end of the bargain as well.

When I told my mother, she was not happy to hear the news. I remember going to talk to her at her place of employment and while I was in my car I heard a small voice say "don't do it, don't marry him." I ran into her office and told her I heard the Holy Spirit tell me not to go forward with the marriage. But that wasn't enough to stop me. I wanted this man and I was praying that this marriage would solidify our relationship. We would have the happy family that I wanted.

Let's pause here. Women- there is nothing you can ever do to change or keep a man. If he wants to be with other women that is what he will do. Marrying him or having kids with him may not change him. It is up to him to WANT to change.

Then what happens when you have the man who doesn't know how to be a father or a husband because he has no examples? What can you expect then? This is where we make a huge mistake. We are then left with raising children due to failed relationships.

Some women think that they can raise a man. No! We can teach our sons how to be respectable and respectful but we could NEVER teach them how to be men! With there being so many single mothers parenting young boys, we will constantly be addressing this issue.

My mother and those close to me refused to attend the ceremony. We went to the Justice of Peace and were married by the town's clerk. Life was life. Nothing changed. We still argued and fought and it remained on repeat.

The following year wasn't a bad year for me. I continued my education and graduated from a local community college with high marks. I was invited to join the Phi Teta Kappa Honor society because of my grades that I achieved during my time at the college. Obviously, I worked very hard to achieve these grades. I cannot recall how I was able to pull it off; having three small children and barely any help, besides the grace of God!

I know that I had a drive to finish my education and be a role model to my children. I felt that I could not tell them education is important without have a solid educational background. So I worked until the wee hours of the night. I worked until my eyes burned and the sun was coming up. My children would go to bed and they would wake up and I was back at the computer finishing papers and turning in assignments.

Since I never walked the stage in high school, it was very important for me that I walked across the stage.-and that I did. I can remember feeling so proud of myself, having such a feeling of accomplishment. It was a feeling I never had before. It was foreign to me but it was something that I would soon begin to crave the feeling of accomplishment, the feeling of being proud of myself, the feeling that I, LaKecia had done something right!

Not only was I proud of myself but other people were proud of me too. My daddy drove to the ceremony with my step-mom to see me walk the stage. I would never forget that day! My daddy was there to witness this and the rest of my family was there to support me. What a wonderful occasion it was for me.

This day for me was a REDEFINING moment! It changed how I felt about myself. I began to take pride in me. I began to look at myself in the mirror a little longer. I began to think twice about what I would wear for the day and what I wore out of the house. I began to think about ME more and not just the kids and the man I was with. I put together a five year plan and I wanted to see myself reach the goals that I set.

I began to take on a new lease in life for myself. I WANTED to feel better about myself. I wanted to look better. I still hadn't lost all of the baby weight but I found myself wanting to lose it. I believe if you look better you will feel better! So I started to work on me.

I started with simple things like getting manicures and pedicures. I began to get my hair done and go for waxes. I began to take better care of myself. I realized that I had let myself go by being so occupied with the relationship and my children but I knew I wanted to do better.

Ladies, self-care is so important. It makes us feel better. Looking better makes you feel better. As women, we can become so fixated on helping someone else that we forget about ourselves. We take care of everybody: our children, our husbands, our friends and even our churches. But we do not take the time to take care of ourselves.

Take some time out during the week to go for coffee by yourself. I used to sit in Barnes and Noble Bookstore by myself with a latte from Starbucks. I loved it. Being out of the house with no screaming kids or husband is needed!

Don't take it for granted. Take time to see your doctor and your dentist. Take time to take care of you!

God started to work on my confidence. I had an *aura* about myself. My demeanor changed. I started to walk with my head held high. I was never conceited or arrogant but I began to think like I was worth something. To this day, people look at me and they get the wrong idea. They look at my outward appearance and think that I must feel that I am better than others.

They look at me and think that I have a haughty look. When in actuality, I am the direct opposite. I firmly believe that we should not think ourselves more than what we truly are. There is nothing wrong with looking good. My anointing is not based on how I look. I have been in places where I am ministering and exhorting and people are so busy looking at me, trying to figure me out, that they miss what God is saying and how he is moving.

A wise woman told me that I should not feel guilty about what God has blessed me with. Yes beauty is fleeting; however God has blessed me with something that *attracts* people. What they see when they look at me, allows me access to different platforms. It allows me a door to preach and minister God's word.

I will never be ashamed of where He has brought me and what I had to go through to walk as confidently as I do. Believe it or not, it has taken years for me to become confident in who I am. It was a process for me. Let it be a process for you. Because of out of your ashes you are being refined, you are being made beautiful!

A goal of mines was to own a home for my children, a place that no one would take away from us, a place where my kids could have their own backyard and play safely. So in 2006, I purchased my first house. This brought me great pride. Most people my age were not home owners. It was another great accomplishment.

I started on my Bachelor's degree right away. I enrolled in an online University that accepted life experience as credit providing you could expound in writing the relationship. I worked diligently as I had previously to earn my Associate's degree.

During this time, my marriage began to have trouble. I began to hear rumors again about other women. I remember going to a softball game with him and the boys and a woman that I didn't know, approached me while he was playing in the game.

I was standing watching my kids play with some of the other kids and she was watching her son as well. We struck up a conversation about the children. Then she said it was a pleasure to finally meet his (my husband's) wife. She told me that he had brought another woman to this games and practices.

I wasn't one to just talk to someone about my personal life but of course, I wanted to hear what else she had to say. So I remember asking her how she knew it wasn't one of his family members or a friend. She apologized for appearing to be nosey, but her interest was piqued because she had heard he was married to the mother of his sons, but this woman was white and she watched them greet with a kiss and often leave together.

Well ok! That did it for me. I do not remember even getting through the game. I was fuming. I trusted him! As I studied in school, I honestly believed we were okay! I thought he was being faithful.

After all we said we would NOT do?! Apparently, his word was not enough, even as it pertained to our marriage. But I should know better!! All these years being together and I KNOW this man is a compulsive liar.

Why would I trust one word that he said? But I held it... I held onto what the lady told me. I wanted more proof. I could not see myself ending my marriage because of something that I did not witness myself. I knew in my heart that if it was true and able to be proven I was going to finally walk away from this relationship.

I watched him. I watched him slowly begin to go back out to the clubs. I watched how he began to go back to the casino and gamble his entire paycheck. I watched how he would come home drunk or high. I felt my hopes in this man unravel again. One by One.

I watched how he would take certain phone calls out the room or send them straight to voicemail. I watched how he would lock his cell with a passcode and then turn it off at night. I watched how his whole demeanor began to change towards me. He was no longer passionate or affectionate. He stopped sleeping with me, Again.

He was no longer at home with the children and me, but he made excuses for being out of the house the majority of the day and night. He would come back home late at night, reeking of alcohol. I watched people whispering. When he did take me out to a movie or to a club, I watched the women and the men and the way they responded to him while with me. I just watched and soon I literally felt my heart breaking in two.

[74]

I watched this man destroy our marriage and whatever else we could have had together as parents of our two beautiful sons. It was no longer about my children or what anyone else thought about my marriage. I knew that this fantasy of mine to have a family and life with the man that fathered my last two sons would not come into fruition. I knew in my heart that he was back out there again; that he was sleeping with other women. I knew that I had to start preparing myself for the total demise of this relationship.

July 4, 2007 started off to be another day for me. We were planning on going to his family's house to spend the day with them. He had come in late, as usual, drunk. I wanted to know what time we would be going to meet with his family so I could plan our day accordingly. Every time I asked him while sleep, he would murmur he did not know. I saw his cell phone next to his pants on the floor. This time he did not turn it off. Perhaps he was too drunk and forgot to turn off his cell phone. My heart began beating fast as I understood what this meant.

I KNEW without a shadow of a doubt that IF I looked through his phone I would find exactly what I was looking for! I knew I would find my proof that I had been waiting on for months. I was hesitant to look. I found that I was literally afraid of what I KNEW I would find. But I had made a promise to myself that I would walk away once and for all if I ever found out he was cheating after we married. I knew I had to look. At this point, I was no longer thinking about the plans for the day. I was thinking about how my life was going to change as SOON as I picked up that cell phone.

After a few minutes of trepidation, I picked it up. My heart was beating fast. I was sweating and my knees were wobbly. So I sat down on the floor next to the bed and I began to go through his cell phone. I started with the text messages. All of his texts from the previous night were still there! I was astonished.

Sure enough, there were texts from an unnamed individual who I immediately knew was a woman. All of the other texts were labeled with a name but not these. I read the texts and my heart completely shattered. The texts were enough to confirm that he was indeed cheating and that she indeed knew all about our family. The texts conveyed that there were deeper feelings, at least her behalf and I was hurt. Truly hurt. Then I was angry!!!

I called the number back several times until the woman finally answered. When she heard my voice she was quiet for a second before she then told me that I needed to ask my husband about his whereabouts. Well she was actually right and I was on my way upstairs to wake him up by whatever means necessary!

Needless to say, what occurred that day happened to be the last physical altercation we had. I threw his clothes outside on the front lawn and called for my family to come over to the house. Because we lived in a relatively peaceful neighborhood, all of my neighbors were outside and watching with interest at the scene that was before them. And I gave them a show!!
I was still angry later that night. When I tucked my kids into bed I was still angry. I went to bed angry. I woke up the next day angry. However, on July 7, 2007 the anger dissipated and I was embarrassed. I was hurting again.

I was feeling all the emotions you feel with the demise of a relationship. I was feeling it. I remember crying all day. I tried not to cry in front of the children but I was so sad. I could not hide that. My youngest child, who was especially close to his father, would keep asking for him and I didn't know what to say except he was gone. And I knew he was never coming back to live with us!

I remember going into my bathroom when the emotions began to overwhelm me. I could no longer hold them in. It was like a tidal wave that threatened to overpower me in any second. My chest began to hurt as salty tears rolled down my face. I was literally in pain. I know now that you can feel your heart break.

My heart felt as if it was breaking into a million pieces. I remember sitting on the toilet in the bathroom and saying I could not take it anymore. I thought to myself that I was not strong enough. I was not going to be able to walk away. I wanted to call him right then and plead for him to come back home. I wanted to see him walk through those doors. At that moment, I would've done anything just for the pain to go away.

But I heard a voice say to me in the middle of my distress, "*DO NOT GO BACK!*" I stopped crying and listened again for the voice and I heard it again "*DO NOT GO BACK!*" The pain that I was feeling subsided. It went away. The tears dried up and I felt a newfound strength-a strength that I had not had before. So I washed my face, straightened my back and went back to my children.

The following days went by in a daze. He began calling after a while. I wouldn't answer most times or I would and just allow him to speak to the kids. I told him I was filing for a divorce. He first asked me not to do it, begged me not to do it. But I had gotten the paperwork from our local clerk and began the process.

I was doing well during this time. I had started a new job. The kids were doing well. They were seeing their father whenever he picked them up. I had even started to visit church again. The day that I received a call from the clerk's office stating that my divorce was finalized and that the paperwork was in the mail, was a tough day for me.

[77]

I knew he had gotten a phone call too. I wondered what he must be feeling knowing our marriage was over. Was he feeling relief that he was no longer tied to me? Was he feeling remorse because we couldn't make it work?

What exactly was he feeling? Worse of all, was he not feeling anything at all? I was tormenting myself, wondering what was going on with him. I got the call in the earlier part of the day. The words of the clerk, kept replaying in my mind all day. So when I left the office for the day, I was not mentally in a good space.

I remember again feeling totally overwhelmed. I began feeling my chest constrict and hurting and I thought about the fact that my marriage was really over. Tears started to fall from my eyes. I began to have strange thoughts. I began to think and say to myself that my life was over. I had put so much into this man and now I was lost and empty. I begin to think that perhaps my children would be better off with my mother.

What if I just stopped existing? What if I just stopped breathing? Who would care? Who would remember me? The tears began to fall harder and I began to sob. My eyesight began to diminish as I was blinded by the tears and the pain I was feeling at that moment. I then had a thought to drive my car off the road.

Drive it into another lane on the highway. But before I could put that thought into action, my hand automatically reached for my cell phone. To this day, I know that I was not thinking about calling anyone. But it was the power of the Holy Spirit that was in action.

I dialed a number that I had dialed numerous times but would often get the voicemail because she was always so busy. I called my auntie in Connecticut. I do not know why I called her. All I know was that I was about to kill myself.

I wanted to end it all- at that moment. But God divinely interrupted my life!!!

I called my auntie and she answered the phone on the second ring. My crying and my sobbing immediately alerted her that this was a dire situation. She began to talk to me. She listened to me as I cried and told her how embarrassed I was. She began to minister to my heart.

She ministered to my pain. God allowed her to save my life that day! He knew that I was a phone call away from ending my life and that I could not afford to call anyone that would not be available. I could not afford to call anyone who would not be sensitive to what I needed at that moment. She was my angel that God used to save me and countless others!!

I say countless others because I know now that my death by suicide would have affected more people than I knew about at that time. I know now that there are so many people that my ministry of transparency would touch and assist with the transformation of lives. I know that I am an important piece of God's plan to convey his cause and the Gospel of Jesus Christ to this dying world in the end times. And so are you!!!

Suicide is a health issue that we need to address. Every 12 minutes there is a death in the U.S by suicide. (www.save.org) People that commit suicide are ambivalent towards death. Meaning they are still unsure if they want to die until the moment they die. That means, there is always hope for people who are displaying suicidal ideation.

The body of Christ has got to wake up and begin to really see what is going on in the world around us. There is healing that is coming to our land. Healing that needs to happen so that we can all be whole. We need to be able to see those who are hurting and who are being deceived by the devil and told if they take their life, everyone would be better off. Wake up people of God!!!

I am grateful that God interrupted my life at the exact time that I needed him the most. I cannot say that every day since then has been peachy because it has not. I cannot say that I have never experienced such a major episode of depression as that one. I cannot say that the enemy did not speak to me many times after to deceive me. What I can say is that I never once attempted suicide again!

In 2008, I graduated with my Bachelor's degree. I started to go back to church sporadically. Depression reared its ugly head but in the months to follow I continued to move forward. I never looked back to that relationship. We never discussed ever being reunited. I made a vow to myself that I would never be a part of something that was so ugly again. I made a vow to myself that I would never forget about ME! I would never lose myself.

I would never love any man more than I loved myself. I would no longer be the victim but I would dictate the terms in future relationships. I said to myself that if men did not have to follow the rules of engagement then neither did I. I would never respect another man. I was done with monogamy and wanted nothing to do with it.

As a matter of fact, I was done with relationships in general. I had one other short-lived friendship after the dissolve of my marriage, which helped me to solidify my decision. Call me what you want but I was done being a fool for men. {The consequences of this decision is actually in another book entitled **Pretty in the Pew**}

I was moving forward but I was still not whole. I wasn't healed completely. It would be years before the wounds actually healed. I had so much baggage. I knew that I had so much baggage, but I didn't care. I built this wall around my heart that acted as a barrier,-a wall to keep me from really feeling.

I became hard and cold. If I didn't acknowledge my emotions and my feelings then I told myself I can keep it moving. To FEEL made me WEAK!! I didn't want to be weak anymore.

This barrier enabled me to carry on with life, wearing a mask. I didn't allow too many people to see that I was still hurting. I was still in desperate need for love-but from the right person. I needed to understand the love of Abba Father.

I continued to live my life the best way I could. As I write I am thinking in retrospect about this particular time in my life. I was just living or better said I was existing. I was working, taking care of my children and very frequently I was visiting the club.

I do recall praying more-praying here and there. I was just basically having conversations with God. I started going to church again. I would just sit and listen. I was still lost but in my head I was at least going again.

I was working a job in Central New York at this time and I was very active in the Faith community. My job description entailed me working closely with several activists in the CNY area. Because of my knowledge within my field and my knowledge of church ethics, I often sat on several boards. This enabled me to rub elbows with powerful people; mainly pastors in the central New York area.

I can recall being hit on by so many of them. Most were married, older gentlemen who were pastors of their churches. I would go in and present information to their congregations and I would leave feeling like I was violated. They would send me notes, emails and slip me their business cards. I could not understand how these men could be in these positions, be called men of God and be trying to sleep with me.

I was not thinking about having any affairs or being with any of them! They would offer me money, trips to various parts of the world, dinners, exclusive tickets to shows and concerts. Anything that I desired I could've had- but I declined. I did not want to be in any type of situation like that. I knew what it felt like to be that woman whose husband was unfaithful. I didn't want to cause that kind of pain.

I did meet a young pastor that was a part of one of the boards I sat on. He wasn't married and he was very personable. He was so charismatic and he was very intelligent. We would sit and talk for hours after meetings just getting to know one another. It wasn't long before we were going out together. We were still only friends but we would go out to dinner and to the movies.

One night he told me that he felt like I was his wife and that he believed that God orchestrated our destiny to cross. Now here I was. I thought I was in a good place. I wasn't bothered by any men; I really wasn't even thinking about being with anyone at this time. I was just minding my own business. I did enjoy his company. But honestly, there was something about him.

He reminded me of my ex-husband in some of his mannerism and his ways. Instead of being turned off, I was turned on. Instead of walking away from him when I noticed some of those mannerisms, I stayed. I wanted to see where this friendship was going. I soon found out that if you play with fire you will get burned.

Isn't it ironic that we often attract the same types of people? It's almost like we have a sign on our back that directs certain people towards us. Why is that? I honestly believe that there are some people who are attracted to issues. They smell them out. They can smell your vulnerabilities.

They can smell your desires- your appetites- your hidden lusts. Based on our pasts and experiences, we create *belief systems* about ourselves and the world. We then attract people who would treat us the way we "believe" that we should be treated- respectfully or abusively.

[83]

My friend and I continued to see each other for a few months. We would be alone often which was okay with me because I felt safe with this man of God. Even though I knew firsthand how men could be, I didn't believe this man of God would treat me unfairly. I wanted to be treated like a woman first, but even more so like a daughter of the King.

One particular night after dinner and a movie, he made a pass at me. I was shocked! I really was. We had never done anything but hold hands with maybe a light kiss at the end of the night. So when he began to aggressively kiss me and feel me up I was really not expecting it.

See, I wanted something pure. I wanted something that made me feel whole, like a real woman. I felt that way with him. I felt that perhaps he was telling the truth when he said that I was going to be his wife. It did not even cross my mind that he was using that as a line to sleep with me. He used that line on me because he smelled my vulnerability and my desire for something different.

Let's pause here. I have witnessed (*since this experience*) so many mature (*those who have longevity in Christianity*) Christian men who prey on young naive girls-these young women who are looking for love in all the wrong places, or young women who have has catastrophic relationships before and have no clue what a real healthy one is.

I've seen men who prey on young women with issues of their own, hoping that their issues won't be seen because she is to young and immature to see them. They prey on single young (pertaining to their Christian walk) women.

These are men who are dealing with their lusts and use women to shield them from praying eyes. These are men who use women for their bodies or for what they have seen IN them-men that want to exploit the anointing that rests on women.

These are men who want to mold young women into the woman that they think they need. They have often been married before so these men think they know exactly what they want and what will make marriage and ministry work. Some of these men are in ministry and need counterparts to access other venues or ventures in ministry. It's a sad thing to see this happen in the body of Christ.

Ladies, we must wake up! We have to see what's really going on around us. It's okay to question why a man is interested in you. That doesn't make you paranoid and it shouldn't make you feel bad that you have to wonder. It is okay to want to know who your partner truly is. It is okay to refrain from talk of marriage until you get to know a person better. You should not feel rushed or feel overwhelmed by the prospect of marriage and even relationship. You should take your time and pray about it. You have got to know who this person is.

You should not be engaging in any type of fleshly conversations because they are meant to entice you both. Sex is a no-no. Phone sex is a no-no. If he can't refrain from conversations about sex or he always wants to touch on you, then he lacks discipline in that area. And if he lacks discipline in that area, you WILL see the lack of discipline in other areas of his life. If he is willing to compromise NOW, then what would he be willing to compromise later?

When my friend crossed the line, I was not ready or prepared for it. However, I found myself going with it because I was afraid that I would lose what I thought was God-given. Does that make any sense? But those were my thoughts. I wanted to keep this man because I thought he was the one.

Again, here I am falling for the same game but with a different person. The reason why is because I was not healed. We slept together and I felt bad about it. One day, I asked him how he dealt with having sex with me and then preached on Sundays.

His answer was that *"God knows my heart. I am not perfect. I am a man!"* And I think that when he admitted that true indeed he was only a man, my eyes opened.

Previously, I didn't look at him like he was just a man. I saw him as a God- man; a man chosen by God. A man that had it together for the sake of himself as well as those he shepherded. Don't get me wrong I know that we are mere human beings but I also understand (now) that we do not have to sin.

We do not have to get caught up in sexual immorality. We don't have to give our flesh what it desires. I thank God for that epiphany. That was the end of that friendship, and the end of our time together.

As the end of 2008 approached, I was going to church more. Things began to be very different for me. I no longer enjoyed the night life. I no longer enjoyed drinking and partying. As a matter of fact, I recall plenty of times that I would be in the club, with a glass of Amaretto Sour to my lips and I would hear the voice of the Lord.

I would hear him say things like *"I love you"* or *"I'm right here"*. Of course, I would think that either I was losing it or I was very drunk. But I remember hearing the voice of the Lord distinctively in 2008. I heard him more so that year than I had heard before.

I found myself talking to God more. I stopped going out altogether. I wanted to start praying more; meaning I had a DESIRE TO PRAY. I was beginning to have dreams again-dreams that were so vivid. I recall one dream with my great-grandmother, my nana, my mother and I were in it. In the dream, we were all praying.

I understood that to mean that there was a mantle of intercession that was in my bloodline. I would find myself praying. I would pray when I was cleaning my house, as I drove to work, and as I sat around doing whatever I was doing.

I would find a way to talk to God. I would find out that prayer was my connection to God and I had a love for it that stemmed from when I was a child. I found him to be my source. Oh, how I loved to feel his presence. I wanted to pray just so I could feel him in the room with me.

Even though I was praying more, I still hadn't rededicated my life back to God. Well, not formally. Of course, I knew to pray that he would forgive my sins etc. Again, I have known how to pray since I was a little girl. But I had not formally done so. I didn't know then why it was important for me to do this; to actually go to the altar.

I do know now, having studied how to pray and how to come before God. The altar is a consecrated place where we make sacrifices or offerings to God. I wanted to offer Him my life again. I wanted to invite Him in as master of my life. I wanted to offer myself as a living sacrifice to my savior.

So the next opportunity for me to do so, I did. I was now going to a local church that my mother was a part of. She was under "watch-care" as she positioned herself to begin to pastor. I recall the preacher wrapping up her sermon and asking if anyone needed prayer. I walked up to the altar and when I got there, tears were rolling down my face. This was another REDEFINING moment for me.

I remember so clearly giving my life back to God. I remember making a decision that I would serve him for the rest of my days. And at that moment, there was such clarity for me! All that I had ever searched for, had ever wanted was in THIS moment. I had been searching for so long. I had been longing for someone or something to fill this void for so long.

All I ever wanted was to be loved, to be accepted, to be cherished and to feel valuable. And at that moment, I felt ALL of that and then some. The love of Abba Father is and has always been so overwhelming to me! To know that He loved me through my most horrific experiences is so overwhelming. Knowing that He loved me when I couldn't love myself is overwhelming.

Knowing how He continued to pursue me until I finally stopped running was overwhelming,-overwhelming in such a good way!! That moment in my life was one that I will never forget.

In 2009, my mother started her church and I was faithful to her ministry. However there was so much work that I needed! There was such a process that I had to go through. Many things that I was used to doing did not just stop. Even when I had a desire for them to stop they didn't because I had learned behaviors with NO DISCIPLINE.

There were times that I slipped up. I made bad decisions. I made bad choices. I did try to have friendships with men after that. I tried not to do things the way I would normally do. But I wasn't ready. I was not ready to date because I still had issues in my flesh. I had a hard time with that. So many people think that when they give their lives to God, and accept salvation that every bad thing would dissipate. Salvation is free but there is a price to pay to be Holy. There is a price called sacrifice.

You still need to be delivered. Your appetites and desires have to change. How do you change? You have to become filled with the Holy Spirit so he can assist and empower you to walk the right way-to flee from sin. You have to read your Word and meditate on it daily. David said *"Thy word have I hid in my heart, that I might not sin against thee."* (Psalms 119:11)

When I came back to God the issues that I dealt with before seemed to roar to life. The very things that you have trouble with prior to, do not go away. It is still there and you have got to deal with it. If you had issues in your flesh before, you will continue to have issues in your flesh until you get delivered.

There are so many clergy and ministers of the Gospel that have issues in their flesh. They have no discipline. The evidence of this is multiple marriages, affairs, perversion, and several other outcomes.

Again, we try so hard to help others but we don't take the time out to help ourselves. We have issues that we do not deal with or address accordingly. We do not deal with our sexual stuff!!! Be transparent with God. Go before God NAKED! Ask him to purge you and cleanse you. Ask him to remove the residue from your past, off your life.

When people look at you, you want them to see the glory of God, not your pasts and the things you have been through. *"Who may ascend into the hill of the LORD? And who may stand in His holy place? He who has clean hands and a pure heart, who has not lifted up his soul to falsehood and has not sworn deceitfully. He shall receive a blessing from the LORD And righteousness from the God of his salvation"* (Psalms 24:3-4)

I was not looking for a relationship but I was not delivered from my issues. I still felt that I needed someone with me to feel good about myself. I was going through my process and I knew better. As previously stated, my confidence was built over time. I had to be healed from myself first.

I needed healing in my soul, in my thoughts and my heart. What a long drawn out process this was for me. I had to really learn how to love myself. When I learned how to do that, it was no longer about me giving my prize possession to a man I was not married to. When I learned how valuable I was, I stopped looking for gratification elsewhere.

With prayer and fasting *("Howbeit this kind goeth not out but by prayer and fasting" (Matthew 17:21.)* I began to see results. I began to esteem myself even the more. As mentioned previously, I started to take better care of myself. My dress style evolved and for a time, I was the girl who wore the longer skirts.

I was the one who wore the shirts with a crew neck or a collar. I didn't want to be reminded of who I used to be. I was evolving in the inside and so it showed up on the outside. This style of dress would eventually change as I became more dedicated to God and developed more discipline and a desire for the things of God and not flesh. The Holy Spirit was teaching and training me during this time.

I didn't have to flaunt my body to feel that I was pretty. He was teaching me to be modest in my apparel. I didn't need any man looking at me because I could not handle the attention. I was not strong enough. How many of you women have been there?

As I was being healed, I blossomed. I had begun to get more involved in ministry. I involved myself on the prayer/intercessory team. I found a niche with prayer. Praying made me feel special. I would pray until I felt the presence of God.

There is nothing like the presence of God. I never get used to his presence. I am one who always cry when he blesses me with his presence. Since I love being there (in his presence) I found myself praying even more. I was filled with the Holy Spirit in 2009 with the evidence of speaking in tongues.

During this time of development and being DEFINED, I was holding my head up high. I was taking time to deal with me. I didn't mind being alone. It was just my children and I. I stayed to myself most of the time.
However, I was called mean, and arrogant by church folk. I resented that. Life had made me bitter and mean.

But I was not arrogant. I had been through a lot and I was dealing with me. I was learning how to be confident in who God made me to be. I didn't understand why I was being called conceited and arrogant- especially since there was a time that I didn't even love myself.
Now I was loving on me and was able to really love others. I was constantly talked about.

It seemed like folk would remember everything about what I USED to do but could not give me credit for what I was doing now. Every male I talked to, folk thought I was trying to get with them and it wasn't the case. I was judged for everything I did. It was like living in a fish bowl.

The fact that my mother was a pillar in the community and everyone knew her didn't help. Here I was living in this small town and everyone THOUGHT they knew my business.
Being the introvert that I am naturally, this affected me. I didn't want to come out of my shell. I went to church with my mother for ministry.

My past hung over my head like a black cloud. It followed me wherever I went. I focused more on bettering myself and I continued with school for my Master's degree while raising my three sons.

In 2009, while attending my mother's women ministry on a Friday night, a few young women and myself decided to go back to my home. Once there we had discussion about doing things for us as young women. We decided to start a group.

We were going to call it a sisterhood; a sorority-We called it YWOP (Young Women of Praise). We started out with nine young women but this number would change throughout the years. I was very hesitant about this ministry. I did feel that I had so much to give to these women but yet I was skeptical. I did not want to be transparent. I felt that if I really told them what I had gone through then they would lose all respect for me.

Somehow, I became the leader in this group. I didn't want the positon. Again, I didn't feel qualified even though I had so much to give them. I was afraid to lead. I was afraid of the expectations. I knew that the expectations would be even greater for me as the president or leader of these group of women.

What if I let these women down? What if messed up again? I would make a mockery out of them, out of the group. I was so unsure. "To whom much is given much is required." But as I shared my worries with a few of those I trusted, they encouraged me to take the lead. My mother backed me 100%, so I pressed forward.

Through YWOP I came in contact with lots of women from all aspects of life. For some reason young women seemed to gravitate towards me. Maybe it was my transparency that I finally got comfortable with. Maybe it was my ability to actually see them, see their world and really understand and empathize with what they were going through.

They trusted me. They wanted to hear what I had to say. It was almost like they were waiting for me to say something. I felt like I wanted to have something to say just because they were listening! My passion for working with women was born through YWOP.

I recall meeting this one young lady who was hurting so badly mentally and emotionally. All I wanted to do was to help her. She took to my children and me immediately after we met. I remember just doing simple things with her that would get her to open up to me.

We built a rapport like none other. Eventually she would talk and tell her story. I was blown away with the things that she saw growing up in the hood. I thought I had it rough but at that point, I knew there were so many women who had it worse than I did.

Sometimes we get so caught up in what is going on with us, that we really think what we are going through has GOT to be the worse. I was wrong. Hearing her testimony showed me the need for more ministry to hurting women.

Needless to say, I took her under my wing. I have watched her morph right in front of me. I watched as God saved her and began to deliver her from so many issues as He did with me. I watched as her desire for God grew. I watched how God literally began to change her.

As God worked in her spiritually, we worked together to address some of the natural things she had going on. Sooner than later she became the most trusted and the most loyal friend that I would ever have. This meant a lot to me because while God worked on her, he worked on me by using her.

We are tightly knit like David and Johnathan. God used her to heal my broken area in friendship. Never had I imagined that I would have someone (a female) that close me after what I had experienced with other women. God is amazing. We may never understand how He works but be grateful for Him working!

I was really involved in ministry at this point-doing my best and trying to live right. I was losing friends along the way. It had turned out to be some kind of journey but my YWOP sisters were right there. We were often having sleep overs and dinner dates. We were very active in ministry ourselves but we knew that we needed time to just be young women!
So we ate pizza, stayed up most the night, played card and board games and any other thing that we wanted to do while still living holy.

I was enjoying this life. However, there were times at night in which I was lonely. No matter how many of my sisters were sleeping in my living room, I went to bed by myself. One night after prayer, I found myself journaling.

I wrote a letter to God with specifications of my husband. I was specific enough to include his height and his dark skin. I was specific enough to ask that we grow in ministry together and that he would be a God-fearing man that loved my children and me. I wanted this man to really love me (**LaKecia**), with all my quirks and my flaws.

I knew that whoever God sent would have to be a tough man because I was a piece of work. I knew he would be in ministry and I was okay with that. I wanted someone who would develop and tutor me-some one that would pour into my spirit and stimulate my mind at the same time.

And I wanted to be attracted to my husband! That may sound funny but I have met women who has married because "God said so", and are not attracted to their spouses at all. I didn't care what anyone else said about him I needed to be attracted to my husband. And so I put this letter in my Bible and went to bed. My desires were given to God.

[94]

The year 2010 was an interesting one- a great one. I was now a supervisor at a local not for profit agency. The position was very lucrative and I was able to do more for my children and the ministry. I was assisting my mother in ministry as much as I could.

I was on the praise and worship team, finance committee, intercession team, president of YWOP, and still being mother and going to school for my master's degree. I was quite busy. I was not concerned or even thinking about men. My letter to God stayed in my Bible though. I would glance at it briefly when I opened my Bible but I can honestly say that I was not thinking about being in a relationship.

However, I was starting to receive prophetic words that my husband was coming. Well I thought that I was some years away from this occurring. I was busy about my Father's business. I had also received a diagnosis from my neurologist that I had a tumor on my pituitary gland.
I had started to have very bad headaches and blurred vision prior to this diagnosis. I was more irritable than usual. I was very tired most days and sluggish. But I kept on with doing what I have learned to love to do-ministry.

One night our church went to fellowship with another church. I had a horrible headache that day that would not let up. No matter what medicine I took, it just would not quit. I remember sitting in the front with my mother. The service was high and the Spirit was moving. I happened to look up and see this man staring at me. I will never forget. He had on a gold suit with rimmed glasses on. He was dark skinned and his head was above the others. He was sitting on the pulpit with the other episcopal leaders.

I looked away often just to turn back and see him still staring. I was thinking to myself "Here we go again. This man was trying to see if I would take the bait DURING service." I was appalled. I nudged my mother and asked her to look up in the pulpit and see who was staring at me. To my surprised, she knew him-and knew him by his name.

During the offering time, he came down from the pulpit and gave my mother a hug. I totally ignored him. I could see him out the corner of my eye still looking at me while hugging my mother. I stared straight ahead.

After the service, I gave my mother a hug and I went home to rest for work the next day. I went to my mother's house as I usually did during my work day. She was on the phone with my aunt. When I walked into the house, they stopped their conversation and began to talk about the man from the previous day's service. Obviously, they had been talking prior to my arrival. Interesting enough, this man was not from the small town but they both knew him. My aunt was telling me how he loved children and was a family man.

My mother gave me a business card with his number on it. She told me that after church he approached her asking for her armor bearer (that's who he thought I was). When she brought forth her armor bearer, he said no that's not her. She then told him I was her daughter.

He told her that it was important for me to get in contact with him and then gave her his card. I was wondering how they even knew him. Apparently, he had often traveled to visit my aunt's church. I never met him because this took place while I was still getting myself together.

I took the card with no intention of ever calling him. I was not even thinking about this man. I went about my day doing what I normally do. When the kids were settled in bed, I began to think over my day. I went to move my jacket off my bed and his card slipped out of my pocket. I looked at his card and saw this man with the same gold suit on and glasses peering at me. "Nah!" I said. But I didn't think that it would hurt to befriend him on a social media website so I did.

I added him on the social media website and then before I could blink he had added me and had sent me messages via the app. We chatted for a while before he gave me his number to call him. I was not into talking on the phone and I don't think I wanted to talk on the phone with him. But I have to say that I was interested in why it was so important that I talked to him. Later that week, I finally did text his cell phone.

We would talk via text for hours. I found that I enjoyed texting him. But I still wasn't ready to hear his voice. I didn't want to do that for some strange reason. I think I liked being in control of when I talked to him as I could control when I responded to his text. I had found that I liked my new found control that I had going on in my life.

Eventually, he would call me. I debated whether or not I would answer the phone as I saw his name flash across my screen. But I didn't want to be rude especially since we had just been texting one another. So I answered. Why did I do that? This man had the raspiest throaty voice I had ever heard. When I heard his voice it immediately soothed me. How odd! His voice took the anxiety away. He told me that he thought I was not going to answer the phone for him. That night we talked and talked. We talked until the wee hours of the night with both of us not wanting to hang up.

In the next few weeks we talked a lot about each other's life. We talked about dreams and goals. I told him how my life was ministry, my children, school and work. I told him that some of the women I mentor call me superwoman. One thing that I never forgot that he said to me was that *"even superwoman needs help."*

I was blown away, although I did not show it. I believe that I was blown away because I didn't have anyone that helped me with life. I managed it on my own with the help of God. But here was this man that recognized that I needed help.
I was still being hard and not showing any type of emotions. I appreciated the fact that he SAW me. He recognized what I was doing. He talked to me about ministry.

We started to pray at night before we hung up. I thought this was a good thing. I was still not thinking about a relationship even though I knew he was interested in me.
The next time I saw him was when my mother had to preach in another city. He accompanied us there. This was the first time I actually got to really look at him. I came down to the lobby in the hotel and he was waiting for me. I looked him over quickly. He was very tall and very dark.

He was also a big man. He reminded me of an oversized teddy bear. He was dressed in a black suit and shirt. I looked down at his feet and noticed that his shoes were enormous.
I remember asking God "Where has this man's feet carried him?" I don't know why his shoes mattered to me and at that moment. After a quick assessment something registered in my spirit that this man had been through his share of pain but I was moving on towards my car.

Before we left the city, we ate breakfast at a local restaurant. He asked me to sit with him and I did so to be kind. We sat at a quaint table, separate from everyone else and we talked like we knew each other forever. Later after the drive from the neighboring city, he took me to dinner. I guess he wanted to talk more. I didn't mind. We sat and spoke over steak and potatoes we talked about life.

One night while talking, I was bold enough to ask him what was it he wanted with me. I had started to enjoy his company. I started to enjoy the peace that he brought to my life. The structure that he brought to me. Every time I was near him or talked to him on the phone, I was at peace. It was something about him that caused my soul to relax. I now know it to be his anointing.

Yes, he was anointed for me! He told me that he knew I was his wife. That God illuminated me in the church on that Sunday evening amidst all those other people. He told me how he didn't even see my face or the person I was next to until he came down for offering.

All he saw was the glory of God surrounding me. He asked me what I thought. I told him he was wrong!! Then he said *"okay, pray about it. No pressure. If you hear or see something different, we can remain friends. No pressure."* In my head, I knew I was not going to pray about it.

I felt that this friendship that we had was great the way it was. I didn't want to ruin it. I thought that if he knew my past he would frown on it and distance himself from me. I didn't feel worthy of the love from this man of God. I did not Pray but I dreamed.

God gave me a dream that verified everything he said to me. In short, I was at peace with the decision that I was about to make. God used this man to love the hell out of me! He still uses him to give me peace. My husband is like a lifeline to me. This was our beginning. This was the beginning of a love affair that God used to rescue me. This is also the start of another book that will be written by both my husband and I.

God promised me that he would heal me. He promised me that I would be whole. He also promised me that he would use all that I experienced to help someone else. I wrote this book from a place of healing and wholeness. As you have read in this book, God used circumstances and people to get my attention.

God rescued me from a life that was leading to death. I am no longer bitter or angry. I don't blame anyone for my life choices or situations in which I put myself in.

God used the fire of life, the fire of my bad decisions to burn away any resignation about following him. He used the fire to purge and purify me. He used the fire to shape me. **"For the Lord, your God is a consuming fire, a jealous God."** (Deuteronomy 4:24) After the fire, came the ashes.

I was reminded of the pretty phoenix that is considered to be a mythical creature. This creature after living for a while would combust in a fire that it created. And out of the ashes, it was rebirthed and regenerated. This is what God did for me. This is what he can do for you. Like the phoenix, even though we may create our own issues and troubles (fire) in life, we can be reborn. We can be restored and regenerated. Your ashes mean something.

Your ashes are metaphorical of your past. There is no need to be ashamed of where you been, because you are now renewed. The Bible states **"Therefore if any man be in Christ, he is a new creature: old things are passed away; behold all things are become new."** (2 Corinthians 5:17) Don't let your past hinder you. Don't let people who know your past hinder you. When I go to minister in the town where I grew up, I discern that many show up just to see what is different with me.

They want to see if I am still doing the *old* things. But when I begin to minister the word of God and prophesy, they cannot mistake the anointing on my life for anything else than what it is. Let it be the same way for you. Your ashes MEAN SOMETHING! God gets all the glory for the things he is doing and has done in my life.

I want you to understand that what God has done for me he can do for you too! He can save and deliver you from yourself as well as from others. All you have to do is surrender to God. Allow him to work in your life. Allow him to heal you. You can be free. It is God's intent that you are FREE!!

Do you remember the woman with the issue of blood in the book of Luke? The Bible denotes that there was a woman who had an issue of blood for twelve long years. She had spent all her monies on physicians but could not be healed by any of them. However, it was when she came in contact with Jesus that she was healed. She managed to press her way through the throngs of people and push past his disciples to touch the hem of his garment. She was made whole.

This is how God wants us to be. The same fervor that we have for other things, he wants us to have for Him-even more so. All we have to do is ask Him to heal you and make you whole. Then walk out your process. Your process will not be like anyone else's because it is tailored to fit you. It's prescribed just for you.

Walk it out!! God gives you grace to empower and strengthen you. The Holy Spirit will be with you always and guide you. As long as you are a Christian, you will continue to evolve. As long as you live life, you will encounter situations that seem overwhelming. These are the times when you should be leaning on God. I truly believe that there is significance in life's challenges. Lean on God!

Let God do it. Let him heal you. Let him bring you to a place of stability and security in your heart and mind. Let him make you over!! Let him

REDEFINE YOU!!!

Made in the USA
Middletown, DE
06 June 2016